UNDER THE HOOK

HOW ONE WOMAN TOOK ON THE LONGSHOREMEN'S UNION AND MADE A BETTER ENVIRONMENT FOR EVERYONE

LINDA NYLAND

BELLINGHAM, WA

bookhouse
PUBLISHING

2950 Newmarket St., Suite 101-358 | Bellingham, WA 98226
Ph: 206.226.3588 | www.bookhouserules.com

Copyright © 2024 by Linda Nyland

All rights reserved. No part of this book may be reproduced or transmitted in any form or by any means, electronic or mechanical, including photocopying, recording, or any information storage and retrieval system, without permission in writing from the author.

10 9 8 7 6 5 4 3 2 1

Library of Congress Control Number: 2023922727

ISBN: 978-1-952483-80-6 (Paperback)
ISBN: 978-1-952483-81-3 (eBook)

Editor: Julie Scandora
Cover design: Scott Book
Book design: Melissa Vail Coffman

To My Husband

Without your constant love, support, and patience
this book would never have happened . . .
and I would still be lost.

To My Daughter

A Mother's Love

I know you've not always understood
The things I've done for our collective good.
But they were and will forever be
To keep you safe from harm and free.
A single mother's plight is to be torn.
Burdens mount, hope flies,
And here alone. all is borne.
I could not quit. I could not stop.
Your protection is a cause I will never drop.
Now a mother's mantle you too wear.
Is there any pain that you'd not bear
To see your child without a care?
For all those times I was angry, hard, and cold,
In defense of our safety I had to be so bold.
I had to work, and it took our priceless time.
But it was all for you, precious child of mine.
I love you

CONTENTS

Foreword vii
Preface xi
    Becoming a Longshoreman 1
    Under the Hook. 9
    The Reality of the Docks. 15
    Sold on a Ship. 25
    Peein' in the Boys' Room. 33
    Good, Bad, and Ugly 37
    Danger and Fear 43
    Assault and Harassment. 49
    You're Always Late 53
    Flying on Ice. 57
    Union Hall Meetings. 61
    Terrified for an Angel 65
    Welcome Back to Hell 69
    Strawberry Mountain 73
    In the Shadow of the Green River Killer 79

The Invisible Man. 85
World Trade Center, Part I. 95
World Trade Center, Part II 105
Change of Plans. 113
If He Knew Me, Would He Like Me? 125
End Run 129
November 25, 1996: US District Court,
    Tacoma, Washington 133
Judgment Day. 141
Conclusion 147
Glossary 151

FOREWORD

There are many reasons to write a book and many ways to look at a work as a reader. Linda Nyland has written a book that at first glance might look like a biography of her work life. I see it as much more than that. There are people who go where few before them have had the courage to tread. Linda is one of those people. When any minority is the first, they blaze a trail for the next human being. When a gay man takes his place in a warehouse full of straight men, he is blazing a trail. When the first racial minority takes a job that puts them in danger, they take that risk for those who come after them. And when a woman works in a dangerous male-dominated occupation, she opens the door for those who want that opportunity as well. People who have the courage to stand up to prejudice, discrimination, and harassment are the most important people in our society. On paper, our Constitution says that we are all created equal and that we have equal opportunity to receive the Four Freedoms: freedom from poverty, freedom from fear, freedom of speech, and freedom to see God in our own way. These are the things that are in direct opposition to the dictators in every part of society that want to keep things the way they've always been. History shows us that cultures that cease to improve implode and fail. So these courageous people that walk among us should be seen as the best of who we are and necessary to save our democracy.

When I read this story, I see a blueprint for anyone who is oppressed and discriminated against. Linda weathered all storms by using a few important tools. She didn't let herself fall to the level of those who discriminated against her. She kept her cool and did her job to the best of her ability. She accepted help from wherever it came, from those who had the least status in the workplace but in fact knew the most about the job. She found and used professional help when it was available, keeping her actions above board when her detractors tried to gang up on her and denigrate her grievances.

She also persevered against the most difficult tool used by those who abuse and discriminate—isolation. There is no harder path than to walk through life alone. The first man or woman to blaze a trail against unfair practices often has to take this road. We are all social beings, and to be socially isolated at work takes an enormous toll. It makes the individual question "is it all worth it?" and for most of us it is usually more than we can bear. If you look at Linda's story, you may find the strength to stand up against the oppression in your life that attempts to keep you from your dreams. Things are much better today than they used to be down on the waterfront. Much of that improvement is because Linda and a few other women took a stand. If they hadn't done so, it still might be 1950 down on the docks. As much as a few people in our society think that things were better back then, I disagree. If we don't leave our society better for our sons and daughters, then why are we even trying?

As you read these incidents, ask yourself this. Would you want your daughters to have to go through what Linda went through? It's not just a longshore job that can be discriminatory. Every work center has the potential to fall into a pattern of abuse and harassment if the people at the top are not held to account. It should not be a surprise that politicians, CEOs, and Hollywood producers are the ones being accused of stepping over the lines. When you have control over another's income, promotion, and dreams, you wield enormous power. With power comes responsibility. The easiest way to ensure equality is to ensure that everyone answers to someone else. For those who do not, unfortunately the courts sometimes have to step in. Let us all learn from the trials Linda has endured to make the world a better place.

J. Catera

PREFACE

THE NAMES OF PEOPLE (EXCEPT MINE and that of my stepfather, Bob Lizotte) and companies have been changed. My purpose in writing this book is to provide a guideline for those facing issues similar to mine, and that has always been my only goal.

The details of my struggle are a matter of public record—my case went to court. While the courts are fine with listing real people, places, and events, I don't think it is critical to the story, and in some way, it detracts from the narrative. It has never been my intention to embarrass any person, organization, or place by telling this story.

The court record is pretty dry, as legal records usually are. I wrote this story from my emotions, my fears, and the pain and isolation that I endured. It can't have all been for nothing. I hope there is something within the pages that will help you. My name and my stepfather's name are the only real names in this book.

In the same way, I saw no way to thank some of the people who were instrumental to my success by using their real names.

BECOMING A LONGSHOREMAN

Yes, that's my picture on the opposite page. It was May of 1988. I was ready for my first day of work as a longshoreman, and Mom took a Polaroid to remember the day. I was excited about all the things I would experience and maybe a little apprehensive as well. As you can see, I'm a petite woman and not someone most people would expect to find working on the docks. So how did I find myself heading off for one of the most dangerous and demanding jobs in the world?

That happened because hard physical labor was a reality I'd grown up with. I had always loved animals, but we were poor and Mom said if I wanted to have pets, I would have to come up with the money to feed and take care of them. There was only one kind of work a kid could get back then, and that was work that was dirty and outside. The jobs no one else wanted. So I'd been doing hard work for some time. I scooped manure, mowed lawns, picked up trash, or did any other manual labor I could get paid for. I didn't wait for handouts. When I didn't have a job, I opened up the Yellow Pages of our phone book and looked up businesses within walking distance from my home in Tacoma. Then I made a list and went from one to the other, asking for work. I actually found some work that way!

I used to babysit too. One family I sat for had six kids. Even though I was a young teen myself, I was responsible for all of them, and for that I earned the amazing amount of thirty-five cents an hour!

My siblings taught me determination, responsibility, and self-reliance. I am the middle child of seven, so there were three older kids who challenged me at every step. There were three younger than me, and I was often the one responsible for their care. This situation built a fire inside of me that became a big part of my character. I knew in my heart that I could change my world for the better. My mom used to say that everyone was put on the earth for a reason. Looking back now, I can see I was actively pursuing future careers that would challenge me. All through school, I welcomed challenging assignments.

A recruiter for the National Guard came to our high school. A girlfriend of mine and I went to talk to him. We took the battery of tests to determine what specialties we were qualified for. Apparently, I did really well. He said I could pretty much have my pick of jobs.

I fixated on helicopter pilot. Here was something that satisfied all the challenges I wanted. It was dangerous but intriguing. I saw it as highly technical but fun. It was something that not everyone could do. I told the recruiter that's the job I wanted, and he said there were no female chopper pilots and as far as he knew; there were no plans to put women in that position. It didn't matter to me; I wanted that particular challenge, and nothing else would do.

We left at the end of the day without signing up. He continued to call me for weeks; I guess scores like mine were not a regular occurrence. What I wanted was to be a helicopter pilot, and it wasn't open to me just because of my gender. That did not sit well with me at all.

I talked to that recruiter in 1978. The first female helicopter pilot I ever heard about flew in 1983. The first female active-duty military helicopter pilot graduated from flight school in 1974. She was in the army. I guess I missed out by not talking to the right recruiter. I let the idea slip away, but I kept my mind open for other opportunities.

A conversation I overheard ended up being that opportunity.

Mom married Bob Lizotte when I was fourteen years old. Bob was a good man and a good father to all of us.

A friend of ours, Edgar O'Reilly, stopped by one afternoon, and the subject of work came up. "Bob, you ought to come work as a longshoreman. I'd sponsor you myself."

"Why would I want to be a longshoreman?" Bob asked.

"Well, the money for one thing. You'd start off as a casual worker, and I'm not going to say it won't be hard to get by at first, but before you know it, you'd be making good money."

"How good?"

"The kind of money you'd make if you had a college education."

"Really? That's interesting! What's this casual thing you're talking about?"

"Well, Bob, when you first start, you sit and wait for work. You fill in when there's more work than the registered men can do. Kinda like being on call, although you have to be at the union hall to get work. You can't sit at home and wait for the phone to ring."

"I couldn't work another job to make ends meet until I get steady work?"

"That's right. You'd have to tough it out until you made "B" status. "A" registered men get first pick of jobs, next "B" men, and then casual, or "C," get what's left.[1] The business agent, Barry Newsome, would never let casuals have another job to supplement their income."

"OK. So what kind of work are we talking about?"

"Your first jobs would be manual labor. There's lots of work that has to be done by hand. Containers have to be moved on or off the ships. Logs in the water and on the dock have to be hooked up to the crane. Sometimes stuff that's been shipped needs to be moved by hand, rather than forklift. Anything that can be shipped by sea has to be loaded and unloaded, even new cars coming in from the Far East."

"I don't know how to drive the big cranes."

"You won't need to know for a while. The guys down on the docks are usually pretty good at getting you started on any job. The faster you learn the easier it is for them. When the time comes, someone will show you how to drive equipment like the strad. A strad is an eight-wheeled crane that drives over and straddles a can, or container, like one on a semi, and picks it up and moves it somewhere else in the yard. Or else the strad picks up containers that the overhead cranes take off the ship. The cranes set the containers down on the dock; you drive up in your strad, pick it up, and put it where it needs to be, like on train cars or in rows for pick up or onto another ship."

"Sounds interesting but dangerous."

"Well, I won't kid you, Bob. A man can get killed down there. You have to have your head on a swivel so you don't get into the bite. That's what we call it when you put yourself in between moving equipment and something stationary like a container. But the money is really good, Bob. You gotta work anyway. Why not make a good living for your family? Why

---
[1] See the glossary for definitions of terms used here and throughout the story.

not treat yourself to some of the good things in life that you couldn't afford in some other job?"

"You know what? You're right, Edgar. I've been thinking I'd really like to buy a better home for my family. I could do that if I had more money. OK! I'm going to do it. What do I need to do to become a longshoreman?"

Bob did get hired at the docks. As it turned out, he really loved it. He advanced and learned how to drive equipment and cranes used on the docks. And as his skills grew, so did his earnings. He made good on his plan to buy a better home for us.

I graduated from high school and started working full time. Finally at twenty-seven, I had a really good job at a chemical plant. My job was dangerous as well, but I enjoyed it. I was a chlorate operator, which means I was responsible for running all the machinery that made chlorate, which is used in fireworks, fertilizer, matches, paper, medicine, and insecticides. It burns hotter and faster than sulfur when it's dry so made for a demanding and challenging job. I was responsible for chemical and gas testing, cleaning the system, fixing it when it failed, and working with the high voltage required to make the system work. I was happy there and was also a shop steward for the union, which I felt was a privilege.

Bob had been on the job for twelve years and had been promoted to "A" register. Life seemed to be humming along pretty well until I got a call from Mom.

"Linda! Bob's been in an accident!"

It felt like an ice pick had pierced my heart. It's one thing if someone you care about gets sick and you have time to adjust to the possibility of losing them. It's a whole other thing when it happens right out of the blue.

"Is he OK?"

"I don't know, Linda. As soon as I hear, I'll call you back."

As it turned out, they didn't put him in the hospital but, rather, sent him back home to rest. When I walked into their living room that evening, he was sitting upright in his recliner.

"Bob, are you OK? What happened?"

"They said I went through a four-way stop and hit a car. It happened a couple of blocks down the street. I was almost home. I don't know why I didn't stop. Tired I guess."

"Did you fall asleep? What kind of shifts have you been working?"

Bob looked at me a little sheepishly. "Well, you know how much I love the work. Yeah, I've worked some double shifts and even a couple of triples. The money's good, and I enjoy driving the strad."

"I know, Bob. But you need to take care of yourself. Do you remember anything about the accident?"

"Yes. After I hit the car, I was sitting in my truck, trying to figure out what happened. I must have hit my chest on the steering wheel because it bent double. This guy came up to my truck and opened the door. He had the most soothing voice I've ever heard. He told me everything was going to be OK, that I'd be sore for a little bit, but then it would be all right. He helped me out of my truck and laid me down in a patch of grass. I relaxed, and then the police came and started asking a lot of questions. They asked if I remembered the time right before the accident. I told them no, but the guy who helped me out of the truck must have seen it because he was right there. Well, they looked for him, but there was only me and the people in the other car. Those two said they hadn't seen anyone else, and neither one of them helped me out of my truck."

Bob took a deep breath and eased back in his chair. "We've talked about this, Linda, but I really want to know why you won't come work as a longshoreman. They're opening it up to women."

"Like I said before, I have a good job that I like, and I saw the hell you went through when you started as a casual. It was hard for us all."

"If you didn't have to start as a casual, would you come work the docks?"

"How would that happen? There's no way they're going to let me skip coming in as a casual. It's not possible."

"But if you could, would you then?"

I paused. I wanted to say something to soothe him, to allow him to rest. "Sure, Bob. If I could skip coming in as a casual, I'd come work the docks."

"Promise me, Linda."

I looked at Mom.

She gave me a little shrug like "I don't why he's so worked up about this."

I turned back to Bob. "I promise. If I don't have to come in as a casual, then I'll work the docks as a longshoreman. Will you rest now?"

He seemed to relax and settle back in his recliner with a little smile on his face. We left the room to let him sleep.

Bob recovered and went back to work.

At my job, I worked rotating shifts, which meant most of the time I didn't know what day it was or even the time of day. I was tired all the time. I got in the habit of not answering the door or phone because I was so exhausted.

Late one afternoon, the phone just wouldn't stop ringing. I was working nights and trying to sleep during the day, but I felt like I had to answer it to get whoever was on the other end to leave me alone. I picked it up. It was my brother who lived down in California. It was almost a month to the day since Bob had been in the wreck.

"Linda! There's no easy way to say this. There's been an accident on the docks. You need to go be with Mom."

UNDER THE HOOK

The handheld hook is a symbol of longshoremen, and it comes from the days when it was used to move almost all cargo. Death was and still is an ever-present companion of the longshore worker. "Under the hook" is an expression used by longshoremen to mean you're working in dangerous conditions, like when you're working under a hook that holds tons of weight.

My brother called me from California because Mom had started a new job and no one had her new phone number. This was in 1987 before cell phones were common. A man from the docks had called him because someone he used to know in Puyallup was a longshoreman and the local still had his number. I called my job and told them I wasn't coming in tonight. Then I got dressed and drove over to Mom's house, as I didn't have her new office number either.

When I pulled up and parked, I saw two men sitting on the front porch. One was tall with short brown hair and wearing a suit; the other was white haired and wearing work clothes. They looked very sad, and in my heart, I knew Bob had been killed. I walked up to them and started crying. They confirmed my worst fears.

I sat down beside them on the porch, and we waited for Mom. When she drove up it was dark enough that she couldn't see who we were. I told the men I should be the one to tell Mom. They agreed.

She got out of her car and called out. "Who are you?"

"Mom, it's me, Linda."

She got close enough to see I'd been crying. She started shaking her head and repeating, "No, no."

"Mom, there was an accident at the docks. Two strads collided, and Bob was driving one of them. The cab of his strad broke loose and tipped forward. Bob fell through the glass of the cab and hit the concrete face first. He's gone, Mom." I grabbed her as she started to shake. We made our way into the house.

The men made their apologies and left, telling us to call if we needed anything. They said they would come back later to help with arrangements.

The rest of the night was a blur.

In the following days, we made funeral arrangements, and my brother wrote the eulogy with the help of Mom. He is a minister, and he asked a pastor friend of his to perform the services. The church was packed with longshoremen, and in fact mourners were standing outside the church. Bob was very well liked down at the docks, and it seemed like every longshoreman from the local was there.

We had a reception at Mom's house afterwards. So many people pitched in to help, and we are eternally grateful for all the did. At some point, some of his friends wanted to talk to Mom in private. She wanted me in the room as well. We went in, and they closed the door.

One of them handed Mom an envelope full of money. "We know you have bills, and so we took a collection down at the hall."

Then the other said, "There's a rule with longshoremen that says, when a worker gets killed on the job, one of his children can take his book—his registration—and come to work as a "B" man. It's a hardship case, and that person would come in as a registered longshoreman, not a casual. It's called the permissive rule. Would one of your children want to take advantage of that opportunity?"

I spoke up, "Yes, I do. How do I make that happen?"

"No, Linda, this job is not for you. It's for sons, not daughters."

"A month ago, Bob made me promise that if I didn't have to come in as a casual that I would become a longshoreman."

"I'm afraid it's not that easy. Barry Newsome, the business agent at the union hall, would never let you become a longshoreman, especially under the hardship rule."

Actually, their understanding of the permissive rule was incorrect since (like a lot of the decisions made on the docks) it was made by the men in charge rather than by looking at the contract. Here's the actual text:

ILWU-PMA JOINT COAST LABOR RELATIONS COMMITTEE
Permissive Rule Applicable to Children of Deceased.

A child of a deceased registered longshoreman, clerk or foreman who was on the active registration list at the time of death shall be entitled to apply for Class "B" registration in the same category that the decedent was registered.

As you can see, I had every right to apply for Class "B" registration. Even without the legal permission in the contract, I was bound by my promise to Bob to become a longshoreman.

I let it go until after they all left. Then I asked Mom, "What do I have to do to get on at the docks? I want to honor the promise I made to Bob."

"Why don't you give it a few days and then call the union hall and ask?"

I went back home, and my sister came over to stay with Mom. Later Mom moved in and stayed with me. I went back to the chemical plant and kept it all to myself, but I was mad. I knew I could do the job of a longshoreman, but I was not going to get the job. The only reason was because of my gender. Someone's prejudice was going to keep me from keeping my promise to Bob. First, I was denied a chance to become a helicopter pilot, and now the union didn't want to give me a chance to be a longshoreman, all because I'm a woman. I made up my mind I wasn't going down easy.

My goal after a reasonable period of mourning was to get Mom back on her feet. Everyone told me that it would be best for her if she would go back to work. Every time I said something about it, she would get mad at me. I gave up—she was not going back to work. She was broken inside, and only time could put her back together again. I decided to let her do what she needed to do.

Meanwhile, I needed to work to provide for both of us.

That allowed me to concentrate on fulfilling my promise to Bob. I tried calling the union hall several times. It always went something like this: "This is Linda Wineman (my maiden name). May I speak to Barry Newsome?"

"Sure. Just a minute."

"Mr. Newsome, this is Linda Wineman. I still want to become a longshoreman."

His response was always a scream. "This job is for men! Stop calling me, you f*cking bitch! This job is not for you and it never will be!"

Mom tried to help by asking some of Bob's friends for advice. Finally they gave her the phone number for the Coastal Maritime Association in Seattle. I called them and was put in touch with Ruben Hale. I told him how I was being treated at the union hall. It took a couple of weeks of constant calls. Eventually he told me to come up to Seattle so we could talk.

After talking with Ruben, he had me fill out the necessary forms for work on the docks.

"OK. Now take these down to the hall."

"I can't do that. Barry will kick me out, and I'm tired of being cussed at."

"Well, you need to have a strength and agility test."

"Why can't you schedule the tests for me?"

After a bit of grumbling, he scheduled me for the test, which I passed.

"Now you need to pass a physical. You get it scheduled at the hall."

"And as we've talked about before, Barry will throw me out of the building."

He sighed. "OK. I'll schedule your physical."

I passed that as well, and now it was time. I had my forms filled out; I had passed my physical and the agility test. Yes, it had taken me more than six months, but I had done everything they'd asked. Now it looked like I was going to be a longshoreman, no matter what Barry said.

THE REALITY OF THE DOCKS

I DIDN'T KNOW IT AT THE TIME, but five years earlier, in 1983 the Golden Consent Decree (named after the plaintiff, Deborah Golden) stated that 20 percent of longshore jobs would go to women. It was a little complicated: this was accepted in the Southern California unions, but Tacoma was always a rebel and didn't want to follow the other locals on the coast. So women were going to be hired in Tacoma, but not without a lot of kicking and screaming by management. When the system relented and I came to work as a longshoreman, I'm sure Barry and a lot of the men down there were determined to see me fail.

The West Coast of the United States has always been more progressive than the East, and so new ideas like female and minority longshoremen were more readily accepted on one coast and not on the other. The union on the West Coast was the International Longshore and Warehouse Union (ILWU). The East Coast's union was the International Longshoremen's Association (ILA).

Tacoma stayed ILA until sometime in the 1950s. At that time, there was less shipping at the Tacoma docks. Union members can travel to other docks and get work to survive if they are all in the same union. So to keep local longshoremen from running out of work, Tacoma became ILWU, but in name only. The attitudes of those running the union stayed East Coast. Their attitude was "might is right." It also meant that longshoremen weren't paid their hourly wage when they were in training. Despite the ILWU paying their people for learning new skills, the Tacoma union leadership had an attitude that said, "My way or the highway." Anything written in the contract was just that—mere words on paper. Business agents didn't want anyone reading and understanding the contract or learning what the rest of the West Coast unions were doing. Travelers from other West Coast docks were usually treated badly. The Tacoma leadership didn't want us to know how much better things were at the locals in California. No one complained because the leadership controlled the money: "Obey me, or you don't get work. No work, no paycheck."

All this history put me in a bad position. I didn't know this when I tried to get work as a longshoreman. My goals were to honor the promise I made to Bob, live up to the challenge I had accepted, and earn a livable wage. Other women had become longshoremen before me. When it became clear that women would have to be allowed to join the union, the word went out to invite women who knew better than to make waves. They invited women who would be fine starting at the bottom. I challenged every part of that by coming in on the hardship rule, and I bypassed the normal procedure where new workers were taught to shut up and take whatever scraps of work they could get. I was, in fact, the first woman in this local to come in under the hardship rule. You can bet that rubbed a lot of male egos the wrong way.

In practice the system of bringing in new workers as casual, or "C" class, meant there was a lot of time to get the new longshoremen used to the work and indoctrinated to follow the union way. The exception that brought an adult child of a worker on as a "B" man was so that the family of that worker didn't suffer financially. They were all willing to do that for sons, but not for daughters. The idea that it was only for sons originated from the days when it was a male-only occupation. But as divorce became more acceptable, more and more women had to take on work instead of staying home and raising the kids. It became a matter of survival. Those women who had to go to work didn't have the luxury of choosing only the safest jobs. The same was true during the Second World War. Women had to jump in and do what was needed to build planes, tanks, and ships. A lot of it was dangerous, but our mothers and grandmothers stepped up and got the job done.

We all get hurt at work. When you work in an office you may get a paper cut that means you open a first aid kit, apply a bandage, and go back to work. Maybe you get a sore back lifting a box of paper so you take the rest of the day off.

On the docks you're lucky if an accident results in just an amputation. Too often, as with my stepfather, an accident puts someone in a coffin. In some ways I think the men were scared to give a woman a chance, just in case she could do a dangerous physical job like this—and maybe do it better than some men. Or perhaps it was a holdover from back in the 1950s—the idea that women were fragile and needed to be protected at all costs. In any event, women were not welcome on the docks of Tacoma.

Now you can see how my entry as a longshoreman was going to create problems.

Worse, I had no idea of how things worked when I walked in for my first day on the job. I was directed to Barry's office. I could tell he was unhappy.

He glared at me and yelled, "Collins! Get in here!"

A man came in, looking somewhat apprehensive. None of the longshoremen would dare question Barry Newsome. "Collins! You're Linda's babysitter. Make sure she doesn't get killed. Show her different kinds of jobs. Now get out of here and get to work!"

I followed Jeff Collins Jr. out of Barry's office and out into the union hall.

"Well, that went better than I thought it would! Just follow me and do what I do," he said.

We waited until the dispatcher brought out the work assignments on pads for the day. Craig Malone was the dispatcher for the day. There were usually four dispatchers, and they worked rotating shifts and were on call for evening or night shifts. I didn't know it that first day, but Craig would make my life hell.

He called out, "'A' men, zero hours!"

That was the call for anyone who hadn't worked at all for the week to line up for jobs. Men moved from the common area of the hall to an area behind a yellow line and a rectangular area marked off with yellow tape on the floor.

I was told to never be in that area when they're picking jobs until they call "B" men and then to line up under my earnings. It was a Monday, so everyone was under zero hours for the work week. (The day of the week that started the pay period changed over the years. Some years it was Monday, in others it was Saturday, and so on.) The "A" men lined up and then filed onto benches next to the dispatchers' office. Pads were provided for each man to sign his name and work number for the job he was going to do that day, and then they left to go out on the dock. That went on until all the "A" men had work, and then Craig called out for "B" men. I followed Jeff up to the back of the yellow line and then onto a bench. He signed the pad and then told me to sign below his name.

So here I was, at a monumental point in my life. I was going out on my first job as a longshoreman. It would have been perfect, except for one thing. The men behind me—adult men, experienced men, men who were longshoremen—were snapping my bra strap like they were teenagers in high school. Unbelievable . . . and a small indicator of things to come.

All that day and for rest of the week, Jeff told everyone that he was "babysitting" me. I imagine that if I were a man, he would have used the word "training" instead.

There were several terminals at Tacoma. Each one dealt with different kinds of shipping material. B-Line, Ocean & Sea, Hunze, and Juniper Line all ship containers without opening them to disperse the contents. Containers are loaded onto flatbed semitrailers to be sent inland. The process for incoming containers works exactly the opposite. Semi-trucks bring in a locked container, and it is taken off the flatbed and put in line to go onto the correct ship.

These docks also handle what is called intermodal shipping. Intermodal shipping transports material from one mode to the other. That can be any combination of ship, train, or semi. ABC shipping opens containers and reroutes the contents to other destinations. It also handles bulk cargo like grain or ore and takes new cars off incoming ships and routes them for transport.

ForWest and Cline handle movement of logs. That first week was pretty easy work. The first day, we worked unlocking cans from the hustlers (small semi-tractors) that brought them in so the overhead crane could pick them up and put them on the ship. There was always a team of four workers on the dock for this job, one at each corner. As actual work, it wasn't hard, but it was extremely dangerous. The crane could break loose from the dogs (the slot at each corner where locks or cables are attached) at any time, and tons of weight would fall down to where we stood.

Jeff reminded me, "Linda, never get into the bite. In other words, don't get in between things that could crush you."

Barry Newsome drove out to where I worked every day that first week and sat there in his pickup, watching me. It caused a lot of commotion.

"Why is he out here? He never comes out here! What's he looking for?"

Of course, it was pretty obvious to everyone that I was the subject of all this scrutiny. After the first week, he would appear here and there, but wouldn't watch me all the time.

Jeff told me I was on my own after that first week. I no longer had a babysitter.

After my first month, I came in and sat down to wait for my job.

Barry yelled, "Wineman! Get your ass in here!"

The whole hall went dead quiet. I got up and walked into his office.

He slammed the door shut. "I've been watching you."

"I know."

He paused. "I want you to take more jobs, different jobs."

"OK"

"Don't get killed out there."

"I don't intend to."

"Good. When I tell you, get up and walk out of my office and leave the door open. I'm going to yell, scream, and cuss at you. Don't respond, don't look back. Just go out and wait for your job."

"OK." I left his office and a torrent of cusswords followed me out into the union hall. I sat down, realizing I might have passed a huge milestone. A sly grin spread across my face.

Barry became less of a tormentor, but Craig ramped up the abuse with a vengeance. Today handing out jobs is done efficiently and randomly by a computer-generated numbering system. But back then, if the dispatcher didn't like you or you did something to piss him off, you got the last and worst job assignments or none at all. Craig took it very personally that I had a job that he didn't think I deserved.

"You're taking a job away from a man. A man who needs to provide for his family, a man that deserves the work." A lot of the workers felt that way too. I guess they weren't thinking of all the women who had been abandoned by their husbands and now had to provide for themselves and their children without any help.

We signed our names and work numbers on a pad for our jobs as I explained before. I was now always the last worker to be picked for a job. On the docks, if you don't get a job, you don't get paid. There was no salary. So Craig and the other dispatchers wielded immense power because they controlled your potential paycheck. It was entirely feasible that they could keep you from earning any money at all when there were few ships at the port.

Craig would hand the men the pad for signing. In my case, Craig would throw the pad and pencil at me, and I'd have to get down on the floor to find it. The first couple of times he threw the pad at me, I started to say something. Jeff caught my eye, and his look told me not to do it. I almost slipped up a couple of other times, but someone always seemed to look at me and shake their head no. It was better to take the abuse and get a job than make a point and not get paid for the day.

I learned to keep doing my best and not make a fuss. I also noticed that the dispatchers would never use my name. They did for the men, but not for me. If they said anything at all to me it was "you," not Linda and not even Wineman. I learned later that this is what people do to demean you. They refuse to use your name, making you less than human. You become an object that can easily be abused.

The sexual harassment escalated about that time. A foreman, Ed Gibbons, started driving around the dock in his pickup and pulling up next to me. He'd roll down his window and make kissing sounds at me. Apparently, his job wasn't difficult or time consuming, as he did this all day long for weeks. He finally got tired of it and quit, and I was glad because it was disgusting and irritating.

There was another kind of harassment. Years ago, immigration wasn't the hot-button issue it is today. I never knew the mechanism for hiring the semi drivers, but we did have some who weren't Americans. Immigrant truck drivers would propose marriage, often without even knowing my name. It was obvious that they were looking to marry a US citizen so they could get citizenship as well. At first it was funny, but as time went on it was became another pain in my day. What I really wanted was to be treated as a person. Not as a female longshoreman or as a woman to hit on, but as a plain longshoreman. I wanted to do my job and do it to the best of my ability. I didn't need to be catered to or to have any kind of special treatment.

About a year after I came in as a longshoreman, a black woman came in under the same permissive rule circumstances as I had. She came in as a "B." After she came to work, I wasn't the last to get a job; I was next to last. Now I guess it was "this job's not for you—and not for her either!"

Dispatchers had a definite order for job assignments: white men, black men, Hispanic men, white women, black women, and then anyone else who was left. There were no registered Asian men and only a few Asian casuals. The ships' crews were mostly Asians, and I think there was a prejudice against them. because of that. Some longshoremen believed the Asian crews would take work away from them. Some of the casual Asians had been in that status for seventeen or eighteen years and should have gotten registered status well before that.

In some cases, "A" men would refuse a job if they had to work with me, and then Craig would bitch at me. Other "A" men would come down to the job site, see me, and then throw a fit and say they wouldn't work with me. They would walk off the job and get paid, even though they weren't working. The foreman would tell me, "This is your fault so you're going to do your work and his too!"

There was also a saying down at the docks: "There are only two reasons to be late for work—getting laid or being drunk." I believed it because that's exactly what they did. I wonder how they would have behaved if their wives and mothers knew what they were up to. But there was nothing I could do about it.

Some of you might say a job on the docks is no job for a woman. Some would probably say I should have quit and found another line of work. And I would say to you that this is America, that all of us should be able to pursue whatever life we desire and are capable of and that none of us should be constrained or limited by another's prejudice.

I had nothing to prove. I wasn't trying to interject myself into a male-only occupation just to prove a point. I did not want to be the only woman in a male workplace to try to get attention. Working on the docks was like a time warp to the past. Regardless of what a few people think today, the 1950s were not a good time for anyone who was not white and male. I think we tend to remember the best and let the bad fall out of our memories.

SOLD ON A SHIP

Knight on the Docks

There was no reason for you, son of the king
Against hate the worthy fight to bring.
Royal grandson, you could have ignored our plight
And let us be thrown into the night.

But within your heart you knew the right
So to injustice you brought the fight.
Even banishment from your father's love
Did not make you forfeit truth from high above.

You took up sword of word and deed
And gave protection to all in need.
We now stand, blessed with greater good.
You, our knight, our Robin Hood.

To you, eternal thanks we humbly bring.

> "There shall be no discrimination... because of... race, creed, color, sex, age, national origin or religious or political beliefs."
> – 1987–1990 Pacific Coast Longshore Contract, page 65, section 13

The sexual harassment and abuse from Vernon Reynolds started almost immediately. Vernon was a huge man. He stood almost seven foot tall, and he looked like a professional athlete. No one gave Vernon grief about anything. He was foreman on an evening shift on a roll-on/roll-off ship (one where containers are rolled on and off the ship using hustlers), and I was assigned to his crew. From the start, he was in my face, spitting and cursing at me. I hadn't even started working, and he was already convinced that I couldn't hack it.

"God dammit! Pull these lashing chains, or I'll fire you! You can't do it, can you? You're a goddamn woman, and you don't belong down here! This is a man's job!"

Getting fired on the docks wasn't fired in the sense that you would lose your union job, but rather you were sent back to the hall and couldn't work that job for the rest of that shift. If you were fired in this way, you wouldn't be able to get another assignment for that shift either, so you wouldn't get paid that day. It was a big deal.

"Grab those chains and stretch them out so we can lash these trailers down to the deck! You need to work faster! If you can't do it, you're fired!"

Normally two workers would stretch the chains out and use binders to pull them tight. They were strong enough to keep trailers from moving around while the container ship was out in the ocean, so they were pretty large and heavy. Eight hours of pulling chains by myself was going to be hell.

Vernon got back in my face. "What's wrong with you? Can't

you get your work done? What the hell are you doing here, anyway? Get these chains and binders in place!"

I really wasn't sure I could do it. My arms and back were aching before the first hour was up. I put my head down and kept moving chains. I remember telling myself, "Just do the next one, then the next one, . . ."

In the movies I'd seen Marines in boot camp who got a glazed look on their face and moved like zombies. That's exactly what I felt like. Somewhere in my mind, I assumed that this kind of in-your-face treatment was part of the initiation. I could put up with anything for a while, so I just kept working. My goal became to get through the next hour and then the next. What I was doing must have been something like Zen. At some point, I stopped feeling the pain in my body, but the abuse kept coming all night. And then, just like that, my shift was over.

Vernon stared at me with a look that could kill. "Get the hell out of here."

No "good job." No "you did it." Nothing. Just "Go."

I went home and couldn't even soak in the tub of hot suds that I really needed. I collapsed into bed and was out in seconds.

About two weeks later, I signed the pad for a finishing log ship. That job consisted of climbing over the stacks of logs, stretching a chain across them, and then fastening it down to the deck. It was a fairly large crew of longshoremen with a ship's mate watching us.

At some point I got off the ship to walk across the dock to the bathroom. When I came out, a car full of young women pulled up and started cussing at me. I had no idea why they were so mad. One of them yelled, "We're going to kick your ass! This is our turf!"

I was mystified. What were they talking about? I thought maybe I looked like someone else they knew. I asked, "Can I help you? Are you looking for someone?"

"You don't belong here. You better leave now! You'd better not be here when we come back!"

They kept screaming at me so I left and went back onboard ship to return to work. After I got back, the ship's mate, who didn't speak much English, started grabbing my butt.

"What are you doing?" I yelled.

He looked at me funny and just stood there.

When I started working again, he'd eventually grab me again. He tried this over and over.

Finally I grabbed a chain and stood there, ready to hit him with it. "Stop it!" I yelled.

The crew I was working with busted up, laughing so hard they couldn't stand.

"What the hell is going on?" I screamed.

Finally Jimmy gained enough composure so he could speak. "Ted sold you to the mate!"

"He did WHAT?"

"Yeah, he sold you. It's probably normal in his country, wherever the hell that is. Anyway, you've been sold! Pretty funny, right?"

About then our foreman came by to see what all the laughing was about and yelled for everyone to get back to work. Now the situation with the girls in the car made sense. They were working as hookers on the dock and were waiting for the men to finish the job so they could board the ship and sell themselves. They weren't used to seeing women working log ships, so they assumed I was a hooker too.

I never really got used to the mindset of the men. I knew a lot of them were married and some had daughters, yet their treatment of women was so disgusting. I think it was probably a herd mentality, where if any individual man acted civilized, the others would shun him completely. When they were working by themselves, most of them were fairly normal human beings. The mate must have gotten the message, as he finally left me alone.

I found that a lot of the men on the docks thought like the idiot who had sold me. Jeff, who had been my "babysitter," was a contradiction. He was actually a nice guy and eventually became someone I called a friend. I found out that Jeff was a Golden Boy because he was a fourth-generation longshoreman. He was as close to royalty as you could get on the docks. His father was still working in the union and was not only a foreman but was also known as "the Admiral." Jeff Collins Sr. was as merciless as Jeff Collins Jr. was civilized.

One of my next jobs was to take loads off flatbeds with a forklift and restack the wood and pipes onto pallets. Just like Vernon Reynolds, the Admiral focused all his wrath on me. A steady stream of profanity and abuse followed me all day. "You don't belong here! Women should not be longshoremen! Why don't you quit?" It became a steady drone that I had to tune out to keep my sanity.

This job was long enough that it took us several days to complete. The dispatcher must have been talking things over with the Admiral, as he made sure I signed the pad for that particular job each day. He actually laughed as I signed for the job. "You're really going to have fun on this job!" Day after day, he made sure I signed for that shift, and the Admiral yelled at me for the entire time.

Sometime later, the union put the Admiral up for an award. The reason? Because he was such a nice guy! Maybe to most longshoremen, but to me he was a tyrant.

I worked with different people on different ships, but now and again I would be assigned with Jeff Junior. He was genuinely interested about how I was getting along on the docks. We had a slow job one day, and we had the opportunity to talk.

"Things going OK, Linda?" he asked.

"For the most part, yes. I'm having trouble with some of the foremen because they don't want a woman down here on the docks. I guess the sexual harassment wears me out the most."

"Sexual harassment! There's none of that down here! These are good men!"

"Jeff, you just don't know, do you?"

"Know what, Linda?"

"OK. I'll give you an example. You know Jack Shelton?"

"Sure. I know Jack. He's a supervisor inside the office over there."

"Well, Jack watches me, and almost every time I go into the break room he comes in, presses himself up against me, and tries to get me to go out with him."

"No way! I know Jack! He's married, for Christ's sake!"

"That doesn't seem to matter to him. He's all over me every time he gets a chance."

"I don't believe it, Linda. Jack isn't like that!"

"Tell you what, Jeff. I'm going to the break room by myself. Look through the window, and you can see almost everything. I'll bet you a hundred dollars he follows me into the room and then he will be all over me."

"Linda, you're on. This is going to be the easiest hundred dollars I'll make all day!"

I took off and headed for the break room and a cup of coffee. As soon as I was inside, I heard the door behind me.

Jack came up to me and started talking. "Linda! I still want you to go out with me."

I turned around and backed away. "How many times do I have to say it? No! Leave me alone!"

He loomed over me until I was backed into the corner. He spoke in a syrupy voice which he probably thought was sexy. "Linda, we'd have such a good time. You know you want me and I want you. How about it? Dinner? Dancing? I'd get us a nice motel."

I grabbed my coffee and said, "Tell you what. Let me call your wife and see what she thinks of your idea."

Jeff's face was pale when I got back to the checker's shack. He held out a hundred dollars. "Jesus, Linda, I had no idea."

"Jeff, you're a really nice guy. Keep your money. You were betting against a sure thing. I think because you've been down here a long time you don't see the reality. But I get this all the time, and I hate it. I'm here to work, not mess around and find dates."

I think Jeff moved even further into my corner after that. It was comforting to know there was at least one decent man on the docks and a friend I could count on to be there for me. Not like Vernon Reynolds. On my next job working for him I learned something interesting.

Craig Malone, one of the dispatchers, continued to drop the job pad right before I grabbed it so it landed on the floor. Once again, he laughed. "Have a good day at work. Mr. Reynolds is waiting for you!"

Vernon Reynolds lit into me as soon as I walked onto the job. "God dammit! What the hell are you still doing on the docks? I told you women don't belong here! You know we all voted you down, don't you?"

"Voted me down?"

"Yeah, God dammit! Just like anybody that wants to be a longshoreman, we were asked to vote yay or nay when your name came up. Every goddamn one of us voted you down. You must have a f*cking powerful friend at the maritime headquarters. Barry was told you were coming on whether we voted you in or not. I wished to Christ I knew what you had on whoever's your guardian angel. What the hell are you doing? Sleeping with the CEOs of all the corporations? F*cking hell, I wish I could kick your ass off the docks, but I guess I'll have to work you into the ground instead."

He tried his best, as did the Admiral, but I kept my head down and did my job, one day, one hour, one minute at a time.

Next, they resorted to elementary school behavior in the bathroom.

PEEIN' IN THE BOYS' ROOM

I still hear Motley Crue singing "Smokin' in the Boys' Room" when I remember how it was in the far warehouses that fall.

I did my best to not embarrass anyone or myself, but when there's only a men's room and you're the only woman on a crew, you still have to answer the call of nature. When I couldn't hold it anymore, I would get someone to stand at the door to let others know I was in there. As soon as I was seated, the registered men would push past my guardian, who was usually a casual, to come in and bang on the door.

There was only one or two stalls in each warehouse bathroom, and luckily at least one had a door. Next to the single stall was a row of urinals. As soon as I was seated, it would start. They would come in and line up at the urinals.

"Linda? You in there?"

"Linda! I've got it out. Wanna see?"

"Wanna hold mine, Linda? It's really big!"

"I don't hear you peeing, Linda! Need some help?"

"You still awake, Linda? Wanna come out and watch me pee?"

I couldn't see who was out there, and there's no way I wanted to go out. I needed to do what I had to and get back to work. They would stay in the bathroom until break was over, and then they would all rush out. I'd finally have some peace to finish up, and of course, I would be late back to work.

The foreman would say, "God dammit! Who do you think you are? You think you need an extra-long break just because you're a woman? Just how long does it take you to pee, for Christ's sake? You better not do this next break."

It would happen like this over and over, break after break. They seemed to never tire of tormenting me. I, however, was tired of it from the first time it happened. Then I thought I'd finally found a solution. At the far end of the dock was a porta potty primarily for workers at that location. I decided to walk to the Honey Bucket. I would probably be late coming back from break, but I was really tired of the harassment.

The privacy was great. Then I tried to open the door and found it wouldn't budge. I could see from the couple of inches between the door and the frame that someone had parked a forklift against the door, trapping me inside. A porta potty is OK for the few minutes you need it, but anything more and it becomes almost unbearable. They kept me trapped until break was over.

I trudged back to work and once again got harassment from the foreman. "When are you ever going to be able to pee and get back to work in under an hour! Women! Holy shit!"

"Someone parked a forklift in front of the porta potty door. I was trapped."

One of the guys said, "Yeah, that was damned funny! You came boiling out of there like a scalded cat! Man, you were pissed! Get it? Pissed?"

They all laughed.

"It's not funny," I screamed.

"What's the matter? Can't you take a joke?"

I came to hate that phrase as it became their excuse for every bit of elementary-schoolboy behavior. You would think these men were still ten years old instead of closer to thirty.

Some of the abuse took an even more hurtful path. I was working as a gate checker with Dan Umbarger, a little guy with a beer gut. He started in on me almost immediately. "You shouldn't be here. You know that hardship shit you used to get on doesn't apply in your case. Lizotte was only your stepdad. That doesn't count."

That really hurt me. Bob might not have been my biological father, but he was there for us, he treated me well, and he took good care of Mom. That checked all the "father" boxes in my heart. For them to tell me he didn't count really cut me deep. It was an attack on family, and union members shouldn't make personal attacks like that. Besides, something like 40 to 50 percent of marriages in the United States end in divorce, so I was pretty sure a lot of these men were stepdads. What would they have said if I told them they weren't real fathers to their stepchildren? I don't think they would have taken it well.

I was under a double-barreled attack. I was being pushed physically harder than a man to make me quit and leave the docks. And I was being mentally and emotionally abused by the sexual harassment from all sides. Management didn't want me there because I had forced them to accept me under the permissive rule to become "B" registered, and that made it open season on me for anything and everything the boys wanted to do or say.

I didn't realize the effect at first because it came upon me little by little, but I was suffering from post-traumatic stress syndrome. I don't know that I had heard much about PTSD at that point in my life, and if I had, I think most of us associated it with Vietnam veterans.

But it was real for me. The abuse from all sides became sandpaper on my soul, scraping away the shell that kept me safe. I became hypervigilant, always on the lookout for the next pile of abuse, and retreated into myself, pulling away from social situations outside of work. Most of all, I developed a fear and loathing of entering the union hall each morning to be dispatched. I always knew my morning would start with the humiliation and degradation of being picked last for the worst job and having to crawl around on the floor to find the pad the dispatcher had thrown at me. The physical symptoms of PTSD were there as well. The headaches and nightmares, the neck and shoulder pain—they were all there, making my life hell.

I was singled out by almost the entire union (except for a small group of men like Jeff) to be treated as less than human. Inside of me lived the promise I had made to Bob, the promise to become a longshoreman. Between that rock and all the hard places in my life, I existed, putting one foot in front of the other. It was hard. Really hard. I wondered how many of my abusers could have taken it and pressed on.

GOOD, BAD, AND UGLY

ONE OF MY FAVORITE PEOPLE in the union hall was Etana Kahiau. He was a Pacific Islander who had retired from the military, the army, I think. He had been a causal for years, and I asked him one time why he wasn't a "B" man at least.

"I don't want it," he said.

"Why not?"

"I have my pension. I don't really need to work for money, but I need to get out of the house and to have a little spending money."

Etana was friendly but not very talkative. He observed and he was quite intelligent, although few of the white men realized it. They had already discounted him because of how he looked and the color of his skin.

I was standing beside him in the kitchen one day, and I made some observations. "You can really see the cliques from here, the generational men (sons and grandsons of longshoremen), the yes men, and those that are trying desperately to be accepted."

"That is true, Linda. Always remember what you have

observed here because that knowledge may help you decide who can help you and who can hurt you."

"Where are the casuals?"

"Remember, Linda, no casuals can be down there in the main hall after the bell rings. You didn't go through this because you came in as a hardship "B," but if you hadn't, you would be sitting up on the attic benches. No heat, no air conditioner, no windows, and you would be sitting up there waiting for work that may not come today, next week, or even next month."

"Yes. I remember now. Why doesn't the union fix it up for them?"

"Why? I don't know. Maybe because they see them as less than human and not worth acknowledging. That's what bad men do when they dominate other men—or women. They put them down with words and actions to keep them in line. You can't do that to someone you see as an equal. We should all be equal, but here, in this hall, that is not the reality. You have to earn it, and it's a hard road. Some of us will never make it. I hope you do, Linda."

"I will, Etana. I know I will."

"I am glad to hear this. You have a fire inside of you. Keep it hot and handy, but remember who can hurt you and who can help you. I think when you have the chance to work with casuals, they will show you most of what you need to know. They're learning the hard way, but they need friends too. You can be a friend that can help them since you're registered."

"I'll be sure to remember that," I said and then saw someone who was not a longshoreman. "Etana, who's that woman coming in the door?"

"No one actually knows her name. We've always called her Mama. She lives down the street from the hall."

"Is she mentally ill?"

"Yes, they all think she is . . . but I think she knows a little more than she lets on."

"What's she doing here?"

"She's looking for a handout and a cup of coffee. She comes in to use the bathroom too, although lots of times she uses the bushes around the building."

"And everyone lets her walk around?"

"I think they get a kick out of making fun of her. She seems not to know she's the butt of their jokes. Here she comes."

Mama was wearing pajama bottoms and an old top. Over that she had a stained bathrobe and slippers. She peeked out from a dirty kerchief tied over her head. Her eyes crinkled like she knew a joke we didn't. Dirt was smeared across her cheeks. She shuffled through the hall, pushing through the men and cackling.

Etana greeted her. "Morning, Mama! Would you like some coffee?"

"Coffee! And gimme five! I wanna five!"

"I got no five, Mama. I got coffee. Here you go."

Even though the hall smelled more like a bar than a place of work, when Mama got close, she made my eyes water. I was used to working with men who didn't shower, who smoked cigars, and who occasionally came to work drunk or hungover. But Mama, well, she took odor to a much higher level. I noticed she seemed to look not at anyone but around them or at the floor.

Mama turned to me. "Gimme five!"

I pulled out a dollar from my pocket. "I got a dollar, Mama. Will that help?"

"No! Gimme five! Gimme five!" She looked right through me and took the dollar. She shuffled off, sitting down in a chair in the middle of the hall. "Gimme five!" she yelled to everyone who passed by.

Most laughed at her, but a couple gave her some money.

She was a constant figure in the hall. I felt bad for her and the situation she was in. It seemed everyone saw her not as a human being but, rather, as a subject of ridicule.

One day I stopped where she was sitting. "Hi. What's your name?" I asked.

She looked at me in shock. It must have stunned her that I was treating her with respect in asking her name, essentially honoring the fact that she was indeed human.

She paused for a long time. "Caroline. My name is Caroline."

"I'm pleased to meet you, Caroline. My name is Linda."

She looked like she was going to cry. This was probably the first time in years that another human being had paid any real attention to her. She seemed to look at me a little differently after that, although her demands for "gimme five" still continued with everyone, including me.

One of the things I really missed was talking and working with other women on the docks. You would think since there were close to twenty women working there that I would often have a chance to see one of them. This was not the case as most of them preferred to work night shift. The shift differential made working nights financially more attractive. There were over five hundred longshoremen, so the women disappeared into the mass.

I finally had a chance to talk with Willa. She was one of the first women on the docks, and I wanted to ask her so many questions. "Willa, do you get a lot of harassment?"

She burst out in laughter. "What do you consider a lot? Continuous, daily, or constant? Yeah, we all get that, all the time!"

"It never stops?"

"If you marry a longshoremen, then it stops . . . well, it's a little bit better. Then you have a kind of protected status. But all of us single women are easy prey, every day."

"Haven't you ever complained?"

Once again Willa burst out in laughter. "Linda! You amaze me! This is a union made up almost entirely of white men. You see how it is when jobs are handed out. We're just one step up from dirt. What do you think would happen if you started to stand up for yourself? You'd never work again. And if you're single, you gotta work. So, no, we keep our mouths shut."

"Doesn't it bother you?"

"Sure it bothers me. But I have children to feed. Linda, if I lose this job, I'll have to work two or three jobs just to make ends meet. And then my kids will be alone even more of the time. It's hard enough as it is. No, Linda. I work because I must, and I put up with all this shit because of my kids, and I'd do it again in a heartbeat. But I can't do a damned thing about it. This is my life, no matter how painful, no matter how much abuse they heap on me. I just have to take it. You need to do the same."

"It's not right."

"You're damned right. It's not!"

DANGER AND FEAR

Log ships have their own set of dangers. Logs are floated to the docks, lashed together like a huge raft. They are slung into bundles that can be picked up and craned onto the ship to be sent to foreign countries along the Pacific Rim. Longshoremen stand on the booms of logs in the water, wrap cables around each end, and then attach them to the cable hanging down from the crane. That load of logs is lifted up while we stand on a single log lashed to the ship.

Then we wait for a tugboat to move the next log raft into position. We jump onto that raft of logs, and four people work together at each end to put the sling around the new raft of the logs. To do that, the person in front makes a big loop while holding the knob (the end) and throws the loop into the water so it goes underneath the whole group of logs, then we hook the ends together by inserting the knob through a hole in the lifting mechanism attached to the crane.

My job was to hold the back end of the cable and feed it to the longshoreman at the end of the sling, keeping it from hanging up on anything and making sure he had enough slack to throw it properly.

One of the dangers was that a loose log could be underneath the raft and, when the sling went around the logs, one of the ends wouldn't be caught by the cable. Not realizing that, we would jump to secure another raft of logs. But when the previous raft was lifted by the crane, one log could be hanging down, held by only one cable. It could slip out and crash back down into the water where we were.

The tugs slid rafts in place as soon as the other one cleared the water, so it was dangerous work. Like everything else on the docks, death was an ever-present co-worker.

The only real pieces of safety equipment were corks. Corks are similar to sandals with sports cleats on the bottom side. They're pretty stiff, and they fasten to your boots by lacing them up over the top. Even on the ship, logs can shift, so you must wear corks to keep from slipping. They are critical when working around logs, whether you are in the water or not.

When a log ship was ready to load, a stevedoring company would put a large box of corks on board the ship. They were supposed to include a wide range of sizes in the box, but since most of the ship's crew were Asian and their feet were about the same size as mine, I could never find corks that fit. They always got to the box first. I usually had to try to tie size ten or eleven corks on my size five boots. It never worked correctly.

My first day turned out pretty badly. It was a cold day, maybe thirty-two degrees out on the water. I grabbed the excess cable so the longshoreman I was working with could throw it.

"Come on, Linda! You're too slow!" He yanked on the cable, pulling me off balance.

I fell into the water up to my knees in between the logs. I got back on the logs and regained my balance.

"Damn it, Linda! Can't you get this right?" He yanked on the cable again, and this time I fell as deep as my waist. I always kept extra clothes in my car, so I changed into dry ones at my next break.

After lunch, we started up again.

The worker on the sling was still pissed. "Jesus, Linda! Let's see if you can get this right this time." He yanked on the cable just like before. He was doing this because he didn't want to work with a woman. His job was to throw the cable out over the end of the logs so they could be picked up.

My job was to hold the cable so it didn't swing around and hit him in the back of the head. I was doing my job correctly. He was going out of his way to make me fall.

This time when I fell, I went all the way down into the water. I saw the depth markings on the side of the ship as I slowly sank. It was surreal, seeing the water and drifting down into the darkness. Eventually I bobbed back up to the surface, where someone grabbed me and pulled me out.

The foreman cussed, "Get out of here! You're making more work for me!"

I went home and dried off. I asked everyone who would listen for a solution. Eventually someone told me to go directly to the stevedoring company and get corks that fit. It sounded like a good idea.

"Hi. I'm working log ships, and I need some size five corks."

"We put a good mix of sizes in the box on every log ship. We don't give out extra corks."

"The problem is that the ship's crew have about the same shoe size as I do, and they get the corks first. There are never any corks to fit me when I get on board."

"Too bad. You're not getting any more f*cking corks. Get the f*ck out of here."

I stood there and thought for a minute. It wasn't like this was costing this guy any money. The stevedoring company was paid to supply longshoremen with equipment to get the job done. One pair of corks wasn't going to bust anyone's budget or raise any red flags in the balance sheets. This was pure dislike of having a woman working the docks and me asking him to do his job, rather than sit there and suck coffee.

"OK. That's fine. I'm going to call Coastal Maritime and tell them I can't get safety equipment and I'm being put in danger. I'll be sure to let them know whom I talked to." I turned to walk away. Then I heard some cussing, and a pair of corks flew past me.

"Don't ever come back here, you f*cking bitch!"

I smiled, picked up my corks, and on the way home from work that evening I stopped at the hardware store. I bought the brightest, prettiest pink spray paint I could find. That night I gave my new corks a loving coat of paint. You should have heard the men the next day at the docks!

"Pink corks! Who wears pink corks! Pinky! Pinky's here!"

You know what? No one, and I mean no one, ever touched my corks. I could leave them anywhere and count on them being there when I got back. The men wouldn't touch them. I never fell in the water again after I got my pink corks!

Log ships were exhausting, and working the log booms is just about one of the most dangerous jobs I've ever had on the docks. Only an ore ship is worse because of the conditions. The problem with an ore ship is that it is extremely dusty and dirty. The dust penetrates everywhere. Most of the product is lifted out by a crane using a clamshell to scoop it all out. But the clamshell can't get into the corners and in between the ribs of a ship. That means someone has to go deep into the ship and shovel the product out and into an open area where the crane operator can see it and scoop it. It's constant backbreaking work in a dirty environment.

The man I was working with was a casual but more experienced than me. "Linda, you're going to wear yourself out shoveling like that. Here, try it like this."

He was right. He showed me how to sit the blade of the shovel flat on the floor and push it forward. It filled up with ore and then I directed it to the pile. I was no longer fighting the stuff I was trying to move, but rather, I was using the shovel to guide it into position. It made a pretty good day when I could learn something useful and work alongside someone who also was there to work, rather than cause trouble and try to grab me or spout out sexual innuendos.

Sometimes the harassment and the prejudice made me laugh. I was working with a casual man, and we were hooking up pallets of cargo so the crane operator could lift them onto the ship. As we walked up to the work site, we heard this over the crane's loudspeaker.

"Je-sus Christ! Look what I got to work with! A n*gger and a f*cking bitch!"

It struck both of us as funny and we started laughing. Then we started doing a little dance. It infuriated him, but he was way up there, and we were safely on the ground. All we had to do was look out for each other so he didn't drop a pallet of cargo on us.

Containers did drop, and in at least one instance, it was likely because of drugs and alcohol. One day an operator in a crane was getting mad at me for giving him signals about where to put the containers. He yelled through his loudspeaker that he didn't need help from a f*cking woman. Sure enough, he caught the edge of the can he was moving on the one below it. The container came loose and fell onto the flatbed below. The flatbed was attached to a semi waiting to transport it, and the driver was sitting inside. The truck bounced about five feet into the air. The driver was cut and bruised but otherwise OK. I called for help, and before aid could arrive, the buddies of the crane operator got him out of there and sent him home. He was usually drinking or high, so it's likely he was under the influence when the accident happened.

It was impossible to say anything about all the drugs and alcohol workers used on the docks. Anyone who even hinted at reporting that never worked another day on the docks. And of course, there were no urine tests to see if anyone was under the influence. You were at the mercy of other workers because they were more senior or favorites of a supervisor.

Again, the contract had penalties for drinking and drugging on the job, but unless those penalties were enforced, the behavior was going to continue. And if supervisors were joining in, there sure wasn't going to be anyone reporting it. The supervisors were using drugs and alcohol more than the regular workers.

ASSAULT AND HARASSMENT

It was night on the docks. I don't even remember what I was doing, except that I bent over. It could have been to pick something up or to tie my shoes. I don't remember. All I know is what happened was a step too far.

As I came up, I felt someone grab my hips. Two strong hands pulled me up and back, and I felt a man's groin rub and push into my butt. I struggled and wriggled away. I looked to see who it was. It was Harry London.

"See, Linda? This is what happens when you bend over in front of a real man."

I stood there, trembling with rage.

London could tell I was mad. "You never will learn how to take a joke, will you?"

It was one thing to put up with the insults and innuendos. It was an entirely different thing to put up with someone putting his hands on me. These incidents pushed my PTSD symptoms even harder. It made me afraid to be at work. My neck and shoulders were sore most of the time, and I'm sure it was from stress and being constantly on guard. The adrenaline that my body was pumping out was increasing my jumpiness and grouchiness. I hated going into the hall each morning for pick because of incidents like this. Ronny Sloan was sitting at the back of the hall by the kitchen. I was back there to get coffee, and before I could react, he grabbed my arm and pulled me on his lap and over his groin.

"What the hell are you doing?" I screamed.

It was 7 a.m., and the man was drunk! He smelled of piss.

He kept saying, "She's mine, she's mine!"

Everyone started to look at that point.

I pushed him away and finally broke free.

Everyone started laughing.

It was not funny to me. He would often grab me and then start in with things like this: "Felt good, didn't it? You want more, don't you? I can make you squeal! You know you want it, so let's make a date and head to a motel. What d' you say?"

"No! How dare you touch me!"

"I don't just want to touch you, Linda, but I do like the screaming part! Do you scream and wiggle a lot when you're in bed? I'll bet you do! I like that! Who wants a woman who just lays there? Well, unless she's really hot, you know . . ."

"You've crossed the line here!"

"Yeah, we've crossed a line! The line between you being here and you being in bed with me. How about tonight? Who you sleeping with now, anyway? He must be some wimpy boy because I can tell you haven't been with a real man like me. If you had, you'd be pleading with me to call and get a motel room right now. I'm really hung, you know. You'll never want another man once I've made you scream."

I would run off, holding back the tears and shaking. The way it happened—out of the blue and at work—hit me so hard. What was wrong with these men? I was in work clothes! I was dirty! This wasn't a bar! They had girlfriends and wives at home! What made them think work wasn't work but instead was a party barge and all women were fair game?

Ronny Sloan made a point of sitting close to the door of the union hall so he could grab me as I came in. Any time he had a chance to get close to me and grab at me, he did. He had a laser-like focus when it came to giving me a bad time. And no one ever said a single thing to him. He was never told to stop, never told he was going too far, or never told what he was doing was against the union contract and federal law.

Those men who sat there and watched and did nothing were as guilty as Sloan in my mind. White men as a group don't have to put up with discrimination. If anyone says anything to them, they all stand up and gather around him. It's intimidation by numbers and strength. One woman surrounded by men has no group to stand with her. There is no strength of numbers because you are by yourself. It's frightening, and it's why we have laws preventing that kind of behavior. If we didn't, no woman would ever be safe. Men see us as prey and property. Maybe that's the reason they fear equality because, if they become the only white man in a room of women and minorities, they know they will be at our mercy and they will feel the terror we live with on a daily basis.

YOU'RE ALWAYS LATE

Some of the docks have so much activity that no one can walk from the parking area to the ship. It's considered too dangerous. You go to a stop where a small company van picks up all the workers, and it takes you right to the ship.

Hunze is one of those docks. I signed the pad to work the ship, and to make sure I was on time, I arrived at the bus stop twenty minutes early. It wasn't a long distance; I could see the ship from the stop.

The van arrived and I got on. There was only one other person.

"Good morning. I need to go to the ship," I said.

The driver nodded and I sat down.

Ronny Sloan, one of my main tormentors, spoke up. "Hey, Chuck! I need to get something from my strad. Go there first."

"I'll be late if we go there first," I said.

"Too bad! I'm in a hurry. Chuck! Go to the strad first."

They laughed. We made the detour, and then Chuck took me to the ship. I was five minutes late.

The foreman yelled at me. "You're late! You're fired! Go on

back to the union hall, and if I were you, I'd keep going! You're done for today!"

I went back and told the dispatcher what had happened.

"You got off easy! Just be glad you didn't get written up for being late. I hear you're always late coming back from the bathroom. You're worthless. You know that, don't you?"

Fired. The loss of a whole shift's income. I needed to work, though, so I went home and came back for the evening shift. I would have to go under any longshoreman to get a job.

Craig Malone, the dispatcher, kept the abuse coming. He yelled at me constantly. "Women are all lazy. I don't know what in the hell you women think you're doing down here."

Craig spent his time in the hall, handing out jobs. He never had a chance to see me working. If he did, he wouldn't have used the word 'lazy.' I worked as hard as any man and harder than a lot of them. None of them ever called me lazy to my face. It was a term they used for all women. I guess it made them feel superior.

I heard all the other stereotypes men use against women as well:

"Careful, Linda! You'll break a nail!"

"Are you on your period, Linda?"

"Don't get mad. You might pee in your pants, Linda!"

The broken nail thing was kind of funny. When it was just one of the men and me, they would often ask if I had nail clippers. Of course I let them borrow mine. One time I had a man beg me to let him use my lip balm. Most of them acted civilized when it was a one-on-one situation. Almost all of them acted like animals when they were in a group and went along with just about anything.

But Craig never acted civilized. If he wasn't throwing the pad at me, it was because I wasn't getting any work at all. In between dirty looks, he would pick men all around me and save me for last. The words hurt, and each day, they added to the emotional toll. The PTSD symptoms increased on a weekly basis.

It escalated to physical assault the next week. Craig came boiling out of the dispatcher's office and ran right into me. The whole area was open, so there was no reason for him to crash into me. And he wasn't going anywhere important. He purposely crashed into me and almost knocked me over. He was twice as big as me.

I complained to the business agent, who once again told me I was on my own. He told me I was lucky I still had a job and to just shut up or quit.

So the abuse continued. At some point, you just become numb to constant harassment. Of course the pressure doesn't actually go away. You merely become used to it until something makes it all blow up.

I was working in one of the warehouses where containers were brought from the ship and then we would reorganize them into different groups so the trucks could take them inland (transloading). There was only one break room, and over time, centerfolds had been plastered all over the walls. There wasn't one empty spot on any of the walls. Everywhere I looked there were naked women, couples having sex. and just about any position you could think of was displayed in full color.

Finally I boiled over. "Do you men want these pictures? If you do, I'll stack them all up for you. But I can't take it anymore. I need to take these down."

The men raised holy hell. "What the f*ck do you think you're doing? Why did you take all this down? It took us a really long time to collect all these and put them in just the right positions!"

"Because it is offensive!"

"You may think so, but we don't. If you don't like it, don't work here. What's your problem anyway? You've got a nice ass!

You'd make a nice centerfold yourself, and that's not harassment; that's a compliment!"

"In your mind maybe, but not mine."

Ronny Sloan came on to me again. He was drunk (and, yes, this was at work). and he grabbed me and spun me around to face him. He started all over again with the motel and sex talk.

It's unbelievable men will even have one beer in such a dangerous environment, but twelve packs were common. Snorting coke was common. If you gave your foreman a fifth, you could do whatever you wanted. And no one said anything because the booze and drugs were so prevalent. If someone caused all this to stop, they'd likely be the next person to have an accident.

I pushed him away, just like so many times before and added it to my list. A list that was getting really long.

Even when I got a break (which wasn't often), the men managed to turn it against me. My grandmother was in the hospital, and my supervisor knew it. He also knew I wanted to spend as much time as possible with her. He let me off early a couple of times. Did the men understand? No. They said it was favoritism. Of course when they needed time off for some reason, they called it justified.

Like everything else, it was unfair, and it added to my stress.

FLYING ON ICE

I was working at Ocean & Sea on the night shift. I was the extra man on the dock. It was winter, and the dock was as icy as a skating rink. I should not have worked that night. It was a nightmare out there.

The top row of containers needed to be unlocked so they could be lifted off the ship. On this ship, the containers were stacked five high. That means I was working forty to fifty feet above a pitching deck with no safety harness. There are only two ways to do the job. One way is to work between the containers and unlock them level by level. The other is to stand on top of the cans and reach down with a long pole to unlock them. On this ship I had to unlock them from the top tier. To get there, we "flew" up to the top of the ship. The way we flew to the top was simple but dangerous. The crane has a spreader bar with a permanent cage attached on top so it looks like an open-air elevator. It has bars of metal you step onto, and then the crane lifts you up in the air. It's open at the top and nothing most people would want to ride that high into the air. If you've ever seen linemen working on power poles along the highway, you've seen something similar. The top containers were fifty or more feet above the deck of the ship, so a fall could be fatal.

We used to joke and say, "Why should we pay money for rides at the fair when we have a crane at work!" But this particular night was going to be a horror!

I asked about safety gear, and I was told there was none. I stood inside the cage with no harness, no safety gear of any kind. As I stepped off, my foot slipped. I froze. I couldn't move. The wind was screaming across the tops of the containers lashed to the ship. After a minute, I got down on all fours and crawled along with my heavy, ten-foot metal pole to unlock the dogs holding things together. Soon I was working lying on my belly, and the crane operator was laughing at me with his loudspeaker turned on.

"Quit being such a pussy! What a chicken shit!"

I noticed another worker on the next set of cans was on his knees working. I had to slide on my belly from container to container, working my way across the ship with the wind whipping around me.

Being that high up in the air is dangerous. To be high on a ship, even when it's tied up at dock, is scarier. There's always a gentle rocking of a vessel in water, even in calm water. At night, it's nuts. During the winter in an ice storm? It's unbelievably terrifying.

I slowly crawled from lock to lock, feeling my body slipping back and forth over the ice. Now it was no longer a job. It was a second-to-second struggle to not fall and to keep panic under control. My mouth was dry, and my whole body was shaking. A gust of wind hit the ship, and I hung on as it swayed back and forth. Somewhere down below, I could hear the waves hitting the dock in that slapping way when there's ice everywhere. I quit counting locks and concentrated on doing the next one, the one after, and then one more. The cold from the steel of the containers was starting to come up through my clothes, making it that much harder to move from one can to the other and keep doing my job.

Finally I got all my locks undone and slid over to the crane and climbed onto the spreader bar cage. It was below freezing outside, but inside my rain suit, I was burning up. When I finally felt the dock beneath my feet, I let out a huge thank-you prayer. I was shaking from fear and exhaustion. I tried to keep it all in, but they probably noticed anyway.

UNION HALL MEETINGS

Union hall meetings used to go from seven in the evening until one or two in the morning. There actually wasn't that much business to talk over, but most of the members were high or drinking, so there was constant shouting and arguing. I stopped going to meetings at some point and didn't really miss out on anything. I did have to pay a fifty-dollar fine when I missed roll call meetings, but they didn't have those more than two or three times a year. It was worth it to me. Some really strange things could happen at these meetings. For example, once a longshoreman came running into the meeting after it was already under way.

The sergeant-at-arms talked to him at the door.

"You gotta help me, man! The cops are after me!"

"No problem," said the sergeant. "Go into the women's bathroom and lock the door." He came up with the idea real quick, so I guess this wasn't the first time this had happened.

In a couple of minutes, two cops came to the door of the union hall. "We need to come in and look for a particular person. We saw him come in here a minute ago."

"You got a search warrant? This is a union meeting. No one is allowed in that isn't in the union. No search warrant, no entry."

"This is really serious. This guy beat up his girlfriend. She's in the hospital, and she's critical. We need to find him and take him in for questioning."

"Don't care. You can't come in without a search warrant."

The argument lasted for a few more minutes, and then the cops finally left. I don't know if they were going for a warrant or not, but when the sergeant-at-arms thought the coast was clear he knocked on the door of the women's restroom. "You can come out now. They're gone. You probably need to go hide out somewhere. If they come back, we'll say you were never here tonight."

In another meeting, two guys were having an argument. It was mostly because one of them was pretty drunk and he wouldn't shut up. Eventually someone got him to leave, but on the way out, someone sucker punched him in the back and knocked him down. He was hit pretty bad. Nothing was ever said about it by the membership. The consensus was he had it coming.

Years later, they finally put a time limit on meetings so they couldn't go past midnight. I was really happy about the change, but I still didn't go to meetings. There was very little useful business done at them. What could you possibly need to discuss that would take five hours or more?

One of the good men, Bill Baylie, had me change how I walked into the union hall. I used to let my fear show. Bill told me what I was doing was wrong.

"When you walk into the union hall, your eyes are downcast, and you don't stand up straight. Don't let them do that to you! Stand tall! Look everyone in the eye! You pay your union dues. You do union work. You have the same right to be here as anyone else. Never let them see they're getting to you, even if they are. Don't give them the satisfaction!"

There were men who were on my side, but they were smart enough not to say anything where management could hear them. The rampant nepotism and cronyism would have made them targets just like me. They would start to lose jobs and take home less money. What they did do was let me know who not to cross, when to not say anything, and who was dangerous. As time went on, information like this kept me alive. It was critical that I had people looking out for me. There were times when work really slowed down. Like any other industry, there were slow periods when there was not as much international trade. Storms could slow down the work too. Obviously, you can't unload a ship if it isn't at the dock.

When that happened, we often got paid the same as if it were there. We would come in for a job and sign the pad, and then we'd wait for the boat. If word came down that it wouldn't be in today, we were sent home. If you were sent home before lunchtime, you got four hour's pay. If you were sent home after lunch, you got a full day's pay. However, this didn't apply to casuals. They only got paid for the hours they actually worked.

I took jobs at Coast-to-Coast Grain Corporation when work was slow. None of the "B" or "A" men wanted those jobs. It was dirty and boring. The elevators storing the grain had large empty halls on the bottom floor. At ground level, it took up almost two city blocks. My job there was to sweep. We called it "going down to the bowling alley."

This was not a job you could do if you had bad allergies. Even without allergies, I had to take antihistamines to control my sneezing and the irritation to my eyes. It was one continuous dust storm down there. We would start at the top of the building and sweep every floor until we got to the ground level, the bowling alley. It took all day to sweep out the building, and when we were finished, we would be completely covered with white grain dust. We used an air hose to blow off as much as we could.

Coast to Coast paid a dollar less an hour, but it was better than no work at all. When work was slow, I always took it. Usually it would be a casual worker or two and me. Because I was a registered union worker, the dispatcher had to give it to me before any casuals, no matter how much he didn't want to.

There were a few jobs on the docks called "four and four." One person could do all the work, but some foremen set it up so one person would come in for the first four hours of work, and then go home and get paid for eight hours. The second person would come in, take over, and work the next four hours and also get paid for eight. These jobs always went to the favorites of the dispatchers. I never got one.

TERRIFIED FOR AN ANGEL

I'd walked into the hall so many times before, but this time was different. The cigarette smoke seemed thick enough to cut with a knife. June was standing outside by the door. I asked, "How can they breathe in there?"

"I know what you mean. I don't know if they're smoking cigars or cigarettes, but this is pretty bad."

"Well, I have to make a run for it. I need to get over to the other side."

"Good luck."

I took a deep breath and started making my way through the crowd. No matter how hard I tried, I couldn't seem to make it through all the men milling around so I could get to the kitchen and hopefully a cup of coffee. There was no other option; I had to take a breath. As soon as I did, I felt the nausea building up inside of me. Finally I got over to the other side and made my way to the bathroom. I felt like I was going to pass out.

June caught my arm; she must have seen the look on my face. "Linda! Are you OK? You look pretty green!"

"I have to get inside the bathroom. I'm going to lose it."

She helped me inside, and after several minutes, I managed to get myself under control. I went back out to the hall.

June looked at me with concern. "Pregnant?"

The idea sent ice through my veins. I had recently gotten married and changed my name from Wineman to Nyland, so yes, it was possible. Pregnant! I just couldn't imagine what I was going to do if I was! It would be the end of working the docks because it would be too dangerous for the baby. And if I was pregnant, I didn't want to lose my child. Between my job and my baby, this pregnancy was going to be number one every time. "No, not me," I answered weakly. But I wasn't sure. Later in the week, my doctor confirmed it. I was. That sent me into a panic.

"Doctor! This just can't be! It will be too dangerous for the baby!"

"What do you mean?"

"I'm a longshoreman! It's a dangerous place! It's not like an office job. Where I work you don't get a paper cut—you lose an arm!"

She laughed, "Now, now, just tell your boss. I'm sure they have some light duty they can put you on until after the baby is born."

It was my turn to laugh. "You don't know any longshoremen, do you? They'd rather see me kicked out of the union than get a break for being pregnant. There is no light duty. The guy who gives out the jobs will make sure I have the most dangerous ones."

She looked at me for a while and then wrote out a prescription for me to take it easy and not perform any dangerous tasks. I wasn't sure what good that would do.

As it happened, I heard about other pregnant women in other locals, and I asked what they did to survive. If you qualified, you could take leave while you were pregnant. This was all new for our local, as I would be its first woman to have a baby while working as a longshoreman. I worked with the finance office of the Maritime Association, and they ended up getting it approved by going through the San Francisco office because the local would never have approved it. Whatever works, right?

The other bright spot happened when some of the longshorewomen threw me a baby shower, which I had not expected. I was the very first "B" woman to have a baby in our local. It naturally made me feel close to them, and there should have been a similar feeling of support and solidarity from the union at large, but it wasn't there. It highlighted the immaturity of most of the men who worked the docks.

Having time to spend with my baby was the best time of my life, but eventually, I had to go back to work. My daughter and my job were the center of my world. When she was older, she understood what I did for a living. She drew a picture of me pulling a ship up to the dock. She wrote on it that I am the strongest mom alive. It is still one of my most treasured possessions.

One thing I refused to do after my daughter came into my life was to work on a log ship. She and I depended on each other. If anything happened to me, I had no idea who would be there to care for her now that I was divorced and her father was no longer in our lives. And I needed her even more than she needed me.

WELCOME BACK TO HELL

When I came back after maternity leave, I was hoping things might be a little better. Only two things were better.

The major change was bathrooms. Now there were both men's and women's bathrooms, although in a couple of instances, it was one room with two parts. Still, this was a huge improvement.

Safety equipment was the other big change. It was now everywhere and available to all. It wasn't due to anything I had done, though. While I was on maternity leave, a man had fallen off of a container and broken his neck. It was a fracture and it didn't paralyze him, but obviously it scared everyone. Since it was a white man that almost got killed, we all now had access to safety gear. I didn't care how the change happened; it made me feel a lot safer and I was glad.

Otherwise, things were just as I had left them. I'd been back a couple of days when a longshoreman walked up to me.

"What do they feel like with milk in them?"

"What did you say?" I fumed.

"I just want to know. I want to feel your boobs so bad. They look so full." He held out his hands about four inches away from my chest.

"Get away from me!"

"What! Will it hurt? I just wanna feel. Are they as hard as they look?"

I lowered my voice and clenched my teeth. I was visibly shaking. "If you don't quit, I'm calling the cops. I'm not even going to waste my time going to the business agent. I'm calling the cops, I'm filling out a complaint, and then I'm coming after you!"

He stopped. "Jesus, Linda! There's no need to get so defensive!" And with that, he walked off.

I could hear him muttering in a little whiney voice, "Don't touch me! Don't touch me!"

Because I was nursing, there were times when my nipples protruded even through my bra. So now the men took to saying, "Linda! Your headlights are on!" It made me so self-conscious that I wore Band-Aids between my nipples and my bra. It was uncomfortable, but it did hide them so the comments eased up a little. I nursed my baby for a year because I thought it was best for her. It was hard on me, but she was number one.

The other thing the guys would say if my nipples showed was, "Look at her nipples poking out! That means she's horny!" They probably thought it was fun or sexy. It wasn't either one. It was degrading and childish.

The dispatcher took right back up with his harassment too. I was continually selected last or second to last for any job. Sometimes I didn't get a job for the day. No job, no income.

Craig Malone constantly spewed hatred. As a dispatcher, he went out of his way to make sure I was miserable. He constantly snarled that women shouldn't be allowed anywhere on the docks, that we were weak, and that we couldn't do the work.

Christmas and New Year's Day came and went with no letup in the abuse. In their minds good will towards men meant exactly what it said—men only; women do not deserve good will. Craig's goal in January seemed to be an effort to make sure I got as little work (and therefore as little income) as possible. He kept giving jobs to everyone else until there was no one else left to take one. Sometimes he would throw the pad at me and walk off. Other times he would drop the pad on the bench and walk off.

The rest of the year remained the same, and I must have become mentally numb to all the verbal abuse. The union labor relations council did make a statement that no one was to engage in any kind of discrimination, but of course without real penalties, nothing changed.

Towards the end of 1992, Ronny Sloan resumed his efforts to get me into bed. We were outside the union hall, and it was obvious Sloan was pretty drunk.

"Linda, I wish I wasn't working, 'cause there's a lot of things I'd like to do with you. How about it? I know where you live. How about we go to your house? Do you remember how I told you I'm really hung? You'd be screaming with delight all night!"

Towards the end of the year another supervisor grabbed me in the hall and rubbed his groin against me. Just like before I pushed him away and yelled. I was becoming too used to it, and it was an expected part of my workday. I hated it. I hated every second that I had to be in the union hall. And I hated longshoremen that abused their power and position.

The main reasons longshoremen and foremen got away with so much were twofold: they held power, and everyone (but a few women) was afraid to challenge that power—with good reason. They determined if you worked. And if you didn't work, you didn't get paid; there was no salary. Their decisions about anyone getting work were arbitrary—if someone in power didn't like you, it gave them incredible control over you—but went unchallenged.

There were workers who were on my side and who hated the abuse I was put through, but as they told me in confidence, "We have families; we can't say anything." I understood, and I didn't think less of them for watching out for those who depended on them.

In spite of all the harassment, I was promoted to "A" register in November of 1992. That was a fateful day for the union because once a worker becomes "A" registered, it is almost impossible to kick them out of the union.

I was told the Costal Maritime Association had been behind my promotion. The normal method was for all those who were already "A" registered to have a meeting and vote on candidates for promotion. One of the supervisors very angrily told me not one of them voted to promote me but word came down from the CMA: I was to become an "A" register. Of course that made some of them all the more angry, and they assumed I had to be sleeping with one or more of the association managers. Of course, nothing was further from the truth.

The comments continued with no let up. "Who you sleeping with?" and "Have your pants shrunk?"

But the incident that pushed me over the edge happened in early 1993.

STRAWBERRY MOUNTAIN

As I spend another sleepless night
I pray that He will lend His might.
Lord, guide me through this strife,
These trials in my life.
I rise out of bed and make my way
To doors that look across the bay.
I stand, helpless and alone, waiting for a plan,
And then, finally, yes! I understand!
When I'm truly in need and my fear runs deep,
He sends me help and friends to keep.
I am safe within this Almighty Power,
From Strawberry Mountain I gain strength
and grace this hour.

I'd been working on and off as a checker at the Juniper Gate of the Tacoma docks for years. My job was to make note of the containers as they came in on semi-trucks. I worked the gate with Jeff Collins Jr. Our foreman, Stan Norris, made out our time slips, and at some point, I found out Jeff was getting an hour of overtime more than me, even though we worked the same shifts. I asked Stan why I was getting shorted and how I could get it fixed.

He always said, "I'm working on it. I have to get Superintendent Burns to approve it."

I'd been asking for this to be fixed for years. I didn't think it would ever happen.

One morning, I walked into the break room to get coffee, and it seemed like almost everyone was there. Stan called me over and had me stand in the middle of the room with him. I was hoping he was going to tell me he'd straightened out the pay issue. He started patting my legs and hips, front to back and inside.

I pushed him away and yelled, "What are you doing?"

His answer? "I'm beating around the bush."

The whole room erupted in laughter.

Not only was I completely humiliated, but I realized all this time my foreman was smiling on the outside and completely ignoring my request for equal pay on the inside. It was infuriating, insulting, and illegal.

This attack brought all the pain and degradation to the top, and it crushed me emotionally and physically. The idea that my coworkers and my foreman would belittle me in public and laugh at my humiliation was so inhumane that I felt like there was no use to go on with life. When I rushed out of the break room, I was a physical wreck. My legs felt numb, and it was an effort to get them to move. My face and hands tingled like there was no blood in them. It was hard to breathe. I was probably in shock, and I was certainly flooded with adrenaline. My field of vision narrowed, and I thought I was going to pass out. I had to concentrate on breathing so I could stay conscious. Even when my vision started to clear, my whole body was still shaking with tension. How could people do something like this? How could they join in the total destruction of another human being's emotional life? In a way it was attempted murder, as they brought me right to the brink on not being able to go on.

The emptiness washed over me when I got home. "Why, Lord? Why is this happening? How can these men be so cruel? Why must they torment me when all I want is the same things that they want? Fair pay and equal pay. A chance to prove myself. The opportunity to earn the things we all want in life and to build a solid career. Why do they want to deny me this? How can it be so scary for them to have a woman working the same job they do? Is it so scary that they will scrape away the last shreds of dignity from my soul and leave me broken and discarded? How can they violate me like this and still look in the mirror without hating themselves?"

I said a little prayer, this one with a simple request, rather than questions: "Dear God, I can't understand the depravity of these men and the depths they have descended to. I can't go another step without your help and love."

I couldn't function enough to consider quitting. I would have needed to be clear-headed enough to do interviews for a new job, so I showed up for work the next day, just as I always did. But it was hard, so very hard. I felt like a condemned inmate walking those last few steps to the execution chamber. I had no idea what they would do to me now or how far they would take this attack. Would this be the day someone would finally drop a container on me? Or crush me between a building and a strad? It was hard to take each step, and I walked into the hell that was now my life. There is no way to tell you how alone I felt and how real the danger had become. Each day I truly thought it might be my last. In my heart was a silent scream that none of the men could hear or even cared about. Of course to the men it was a glorious day. They now had a new degradation to use on me, and it continued every day for weeks. Men would mumble, "beating around the bush" as I passed them in the yard and hall. They would giggle like schoolgirls. You want to hear something really nuts? These things happened the day after sensitivity training for the longshoremen. I guess they didn't really listen . . . or care.

Something like this would make most women quit and go work somewhere else. That wasn't an option for me. By this time, I was divorced and on my own, so I had to think of the best way to support my daughter and me. To lose my job would mean I would have to work two minimum wage jobs to earn anything close to the same kind of money. I needed a good income and as much time as possible to spend with my daughter. The stress was intense. I felt like the painting, *The Scream*, by Edvard Munch. I was screaming inside, and no one could hear me. During the day, I was mad, resolute, and my heart filled with ice. But each night, the pain and degradation overwhelmed me. In the safety of my home, I collapsed and the tears flowed freely. There was no one to ease the pain, no one I could talk to, no one I could trust. No one was there to listen to my anguish.

Eventually the pain turned into a cold hard determination. This incident was a last straw for me. Now I was going to take serious action. I couldn't let this kind of insanity continue. I was going to find a way. It was not a desire to get even but, rather, a promise to myself that this was where all the bullshit was going to end.

Strawberry Mountain was my name for Mount Rainier, and it had always been a source of strength for me. Mount Rainier is beautiful all by itself, but in my mind, I always saw it bathed in the red glow of sunup or sunset, and in a way, in my mind, it was the seat where God came down to be with me and give me peace. He watched me from there, making sure I was all right. His hands came down to rescue me from trouble when I strayed too close to danger, and He pulled me into his arms to protect me when it all became overpowering.

One night I was standing at the sliding glass doors that looked out at the mountain, and tears were flowing freely. The pain of my foremen's degradation had come to the surface once again.

"Mommy? Why are you crying?"

I hadn't even noticed my little daughter. She'd come up beside me while I was focusing on Mount Rainier, my Strawberry Mountain. I knelt down and wrapped my arms around her. All of my stress and frustration continued to pour out in a flood. When my emotions were back in control, I tucked her back in bed and said, "I will make you a promise; I will do everything in my power so nothing like this ever happens to you."

Of course at her age, she wouldn't have understood even if I had told her why I was crying.

I may have collapsed emotionally that night, but the next morning, I was determined to do something about it.

But first a dispatcher would team me up with a monster who would threaten my life.

IN THE SHADOW OF THE GREEN RIVER KILLER

His name was Kevin, and if I had to describe him to you today, I couldn't do it. I don't know if that's because I was so terrified of him or because he was so ordinary looking. I certainly remember him, though. We were working a night shift. He was quiet at the beginning of the shift, but then during break—when we were alone—he started talking.

"I don't like women."

"Really? What do you mean, Kevin?"

"Just what I said, I don't like women. I'd like to kill them all."

I froze. We were far out and away from everyone else, and it was a dark night.

"You know the Green River Killer? He's got the right idea."

That year, there had been a lot of news on the TV and radio about the killer, so now I was really scared.

"I think I need to go, Kevin."

"NO!"

He looked at me in a way that made me shrink back from the door.

"I want you to listen. I hate women. The Green River Killer strangles them, but I don't think I'd do it that way." He paused and stared at me, the darkness outside not nearly as black as the hate coming from Kevin. He spoke in a slow, deep growl. He reminded me of a rabid junk yard dog. His eyes were filled with venom, and his words made my blood freeze. "I think I'd slice her guts open first." He reached down to his tall boots and slowly pulled out a large hunting knife. "Right across her belly. Deep and slow so I could watch her guts and stuff slither out onto the dirt. I'd listen to her scream and try to put all that gunk and dirt back in her belly before she passed out."

He pushed the tip of the knife into the table. I heard the wood give way when the tip of the blade penetrated it. Kevin put a finger down on the table behind the blade. "And then I'd take a finger one joint at a time, listening to the bone and sinew snap. Fourteen joints each on two hands. When all the fingers were gone, I'd go to the wrist."

I whispered, "Kevin, I really need to go. Please." My muscles were clenched to either make a run for it or try to defend myself if it came to that.

The knife gleamed in the light of the shack, like the claw of a rabid animal. I could almost feel the razor sharpness of the blade cutting my skin. I imagined the warmth of blood running from the cuts. The blade gleamed like Kevin's hatred was giving it life.

"NO!" he screamed. "YOU'RE GOING TO LISTEN TO ME!"

I pushed myself against the wall so hard I was hoping it would collapse and I could fall out of the shack. I prayed for the nails that kept the wall attached to give way and release me from this torture.

"After the wrist, I'd take the arms off at the elbow. That would be so beautiful. It's what all women deserve."

Tightness flooded my belly, and my face went cold. "Kevin, I think break is over. We need to get back to work."

"Maybe. Maybe not. But here's the thing, Linda. You're not going to say a thing."

"What do you mean?" I asked, feeling the hate of the threat coming for me.

"You're not going to say anything because if you do, I'll come for a visit. A late night visit. Even if I'm locked up for twenty years, I'll come for you and I'll get you. And I'll do just what I said. Right across your guts."

He made a slow movement across his belly with the knife. "Remember what I'm telling you. Don't. Say. Anything." He spoke the last three words one at a time, making sure I understood.

Finally he put the knife away and left the shack.

I raced out and made my way over to the other gang working the ship. My legs were numb and weak from being clenched up so tight. I forced them into action like prey running for its very life.

Doug looked at me and laughed. "Jesus, Linda! You look like you seen a friggin' ghost!"

"Kevin!" I yelled. "He's, he's . . ."

"Yeah, he's nuttier than a fruitcake, ain't he?"

"He's dangerous!" I screamed.

"Naw, not dangerous—just nutty. Kevin won't hurt you."

"You haven't sat and listened to what I just heard! He's going to kill women! Lots of women!"

Doug laughed again. "Kevin don't have the balls. He likes to scare women, but I think he'd piss his pants if you yelled back at him."

"He said he knows where I live!"

"Hell, Linda, it ain't no secret. Lots of people know where you live. Now, get back to work."

"I can't work with him!"

"Linda, you gotta finish your shift. There's no one else, and you don't want to quit a job and lose money. Go on now."

Somehow, I found the strength. It was probably good I did. If the dispatcher realized how terrified I was of working with Kevin, I'd be dispatched with him every day. I went back and finished the shift and made sure to stay out of the shack during break and lunch. Kevin watched me but stayed silent. I don't think I slept at all when I got home, and I checked all the locks three times. I jumped at every little noise, and when I went in to work that night, I was completely on edge from nerves and lack of sleep. I lined up for a job.

"Linda, you and Kevin—"

"NO! I'M NOT WORKING WITH KEVIN!" I screamed.

The dispatcher started laughing. "OK, Kevin don't wanna work with you either. Here, take this lashing job and get out of here."

It occurred to me that the dispatcher had purposely put me on a job with Kevin. It was a dangerous thing to do. I watched him like a hawk every time I saw him on the docks or in the hall. I made sure we weren't alone and that there were as many people between him and me as possible.

Then one day, it was all over. There it was in the paper. "Longshoreman found dead in his apartment. No apparent sign of forced entry or physical trauma. Police will make a determination after the coroner submits his report." Just like that, Kevin was gone. I never asked anyone if they knew what happened. I didn't care, and I didn't want to hear the details if someone did know. Maybe he said the wrong thing to the wrong person, but either way, he should have never been working on the docks or anywhere for that matter. He should have been locked up in an asylum.

I did make a change at home, though. I found an ad in the paper for a free German shepherd. When I saw her, I realized she had been traumatized. She'd been tied up in the backyard of her owner's house for three years. She looked like a terrified and maybe even dangerous dog. I had some fears about walking up to her the first time, but she seemed to calm down a little when I talked to her.

Despite my first impression, I took her home. Her name was Sam—short for Samantha. She was a very difficult dog, so I found a trainer and asked what could be done.

The trainer worked with her for a little bit and then said, "This dog is broken. She will never come out of it. Good grief, Linda! She's been left on a chain and ignored! You will never be able to trust this dog, so I recommend you put her down."

I took Sam home. Looking into those tender brown eyes full of pain, I took her soft muzzle into my hands and held her. "Sam, I'm not going to hurt you. You're in pain, I'm in pain. I need you, you need me. All I ask of you is to protect this home. In return I promise I will never tie you up, ignore you, or abuse you. You will have good food, a warm place to sleep, and my daughter and me to love you." I rested my forehead on hers and cried for all the pain we had both endured.

Sam licked my tears and then rested her head in my lap. We stayed like that for a long time. Somehow, I think she understood. She calmed down and became the best dog I have ever had. I relaxed when I was home with her, so I guess you could say she became my emotional support dog and I became her rescuing human. However you describe it, life was so much better with Sam at home. So much better that in later years when Sam started to slow down a bit, I went to the pound and rescued a three-month-old German shepherd pup.

Zeke learned the ropes from Sam, and now I really felt protected. There was no way anyone could even pull up in front of the house without both of them telling me about it. In return, they seemed to instinctively know that this was their best chance at a good life. Neither one of them did anything to cause me stress; instead they made me feel much safer when I was home.

THE INVISIBLE MAN

Just like a father
You guided me.
Just like a union brother
You gave me history and knowledge.
Just like a friend
You were there for me.
These are the greatest gifts
We can ever give each other.
Support.
Compassion.
Knowledge.
Understanding.

STORMS AT SEA CAN ROCK THE SHIPS VIOLENTLY, and once in a while, a container breaks loose and gets damaged. If the container isn't lost at sea, the contents are often junk by the time it gets retrieved and put back on the dock.

But once in a while, there are some salvageable items, and about the time I was in the market for a typewriter, we had a "scratch and dent" sale from a damaged container. I got right over there and grabbed a typewriter and paid for it. On my way to my car, I was stopped by another longshoreman.

"You got that typewriter? Damn, I really wanted that one!"

"Sorry. I saw it and grabbed it. I don't know if there are others like it."

"Not like that one. Tell you what; I'll pay you double what you paid for it. My name is Bill Baylie, by the way."

I laughed. "That's very generous of you, but I can't sell it. I need it when I go to college to type my papers on."

"College? That's commendable! I always like to see someone advancing their career. Perhaps we will have the opportunity to work together on a ship."

And that's how I met Bill Baylie. The trio of Ruben Hale, Jeff Collins Jr., and now Bill Baylie made my success as a longshoreman possible. As you will recall, Ruben was the man at Coastal Maritime Association that scheduled the tests so I could qualify as a longshoreman. It was probably Ruben, or his influence, that pushed the local to accept me as a hardship "B" when the business agent and the rest of the union wanted to prevent that.

It was Jeff Collins Jr. who guided me through that first week of work and showed me the different kinds of jobs. He watched out for me after that. His concern and guidance probably kept me from being killed.

And now Bill Baylie took an interest in my career as well. At first, he was very reserved. We talked and he often asked me how things were going. I told him about the pay issue and about the harassment and discrimination. There were papers I had submitted to try to get those things fixed. Ruben Hale had helped me with those, but by this time, he had left Coastal Maritime and set up an office as a labor consultant.

I later learned that Bill wanted to help me, but before he did, he wanted to see what kind of a person I was. He later told me that he didn't want to waste his time on a "flake." I didn't blame him. We talked more in depth about the issues I was fighting. For instance, just last week someone had broken a window out of my car while it was parked in front of my house.

"Do you have a garage?"

"Yes, but it's full of junk."

"I would ask you to decide which is more valuable to you—the stuff you're storing in your garage or your car. If your car is more valuable, then you need to clear things out and keep your car locked up at night."

He had a really good point. It took me awhile, but I finally was able to put my car in my garage at night, which made so much more sense. That's what the garage was for anyway, and I couldn't get along without my car.

At some point, Bill invited me over to his house. He said if I wanted to, I could bring my daughter. I found out that Bill transferred in from another local, and as we got to know each other, he told me how appalled he was at how things were run here locally. I was wary at first, but eventually I came to trust him. His wife became quite protective of me and my daughter. He finally persuaded me to let him look at my grievance.

"You do have grounds for a grievance. You merely need to change your perspective a little bit."

"What do you mean?"

"The tools to make the union comply are all in the union contract, the document everyone has and no one reads. I'll bet hardly anyone in the local has read it."

"I'll bet you're right. I've tried and it's quite confusing."

Bill laughed. "The tools you'll find inside those pages are what you'll use to change the attitude of people in the local."

"But I don't understand what's a tool and what's not, let alone how to use them."

"I wouldn't either, but I come from a long line of lawyers and judges. This is the kind of stuff we talked about over supper. So let me help you. But before we do, there is one thing we need to agree on. I have to be an invisible partner because I'm working on something else and I don't want there to be an issue. No one can know I'm helping you. We can't appear friendly at work, and you can't let people know we meet away from work. People already know I'm half longshoreman and half lawyer because of my upbringing. and that makes them nervous all by itself. Agreed?"

"Gladly. Where do we start?"

"First of all, like it says in Sun Tzu's book *The Art of War*, you must know both your enemy and yourself to be successful. Let's look at your opponent here. The union has become an enemy because the men who run it have it all set up so they don't have to think. They make a proclamation and stuff gets done. They've bullied the union into an operation that works on verbal threats, rather than on contract reality. You, as one person, will find it impossible to change minds and turn a whole organization around. So you need to make someone who has the power to change the union put pressure on them."

He had my attention, but I had no idea whom he was talking about. "Who can change the union?"

"The Costal Maritime Association. Do you know what that really is?"

"Well, they pay us. I know that."

"You've hit it right on the head, Linda! Costal is a corporation created by the businesses that run the shipping lines plus the unions. CMA was put in place to be the fulcrum that balances the power of the shipping lines against the power of the unions. If that balance gets out of whack, what happens?"

"Well, union strikes would hurt the shipping companies, or if the companies could get cheaper workers to unload the ships, the union would lose its power."

"Exactly. CMA is there to make sure it all runs smoothly, which means the union workers get paid, vacation money and pensions are paid, and the shipping lines get their products to market without delay. Each one of those ships costs tens of millions of dollars, and to run it back and forth over the Pacific is extremely expensive. Anything that puts this balance out of whack is going to make all parties sit up and pay attention because it will end up costing them money. Even a short delay at the docks is costly. They want things to run like clockwork."

"I don't know if I see where you're going with all this."

"You can slap paper down on the desk of business agents until you're blue in the face. It won't change a thing because the CMA expects union problems to be settled internally. They won't intervene unless they're forced to. And the one thing that will get their attention is a threat to the balance. The threat to that balance in your case is a grievance that won't go away and that will make all parties look bad."

"The CMA will care about my grievance?"

"Eventually, I think they will. We'll have to see how it plays out. You have to go through the procedures within the union to show them you're giving everyone a chance to solve the issues internally. You have to expect that they will deny, throw claims away, and threaten you. Your job is to not let it get to you, to keep yourself safe, and to keep doing a good job at work. If you give them any reason to point to, they'll lock on to that and say you're a bad employee. You have to be better than good. You have to be outstanding. Do your job, and do it better than anyone else. Stand up for yourself, and don't let them push you into bad situations. I know it will be hard, but you can do it. You're made out of good steel, Linda. I've seen it. You'll win this thing, but it won't be easy."

"OK. I'm with you. What do I do next?"

"We are going to take little chunks of the contract and analyze them. If you don't understand what the contract says, then how can you use it to your advantage? You can't. Once you understand the contract, then you're way ahead of most of the people you'll have to deal with. If you stick with what I'm going to show you, it will make you as effective as any shop steward and furthermore it will set you up as someone who can help lots of people. When this is all over, perhaps you can work your way onto one of the labor committees. That's where you could do some real good."

"I don't think the people in charge would want me anywhere near any position of power."

"Not today, but maybe someday. For now, here's what we're going to do. We're going to take a chunk of the contract and talk about it. Ask me anything. When you leave here today, I'm going to give you homework. I'm going to make an assignment, and when we meet next time, I'm going to ask you questions about what you read. I want you to think about it in depth, and I'm going to expect good questions from you. I'd be very surprised if you read something in our contract and didn't have questions."

"How do I understand what I'm reading? Some of it seems so confusing."

"Well, it is. Lawyers write things into contracts to cover a lot of situations that can happen. It's really difficult to think of all the things that can go wrong and put the right fixes in a contract when all you start with is the anticipation of problems. That's how it gets so involved and confusing. So when you read it, you have to declutter it to get to the central idea. For instance, let's look at this single sentence:

> Any longshoreman having records of habitual drunkenness or whose conduct on the job or in the dispatching

hall causes disruption of normal harmony in the relationship of the parties hereto, or who physically assaults anyone in the dispatching hall or on the job, or who have [sic] records of working in a manner that is hazardous to themselves or that endangers other workers shall not be dispatched to operate or used to operate any hoisting or mechanical equipment or devices or to supervise the operations of such equipment; or they shall be subject to such other remedy as the Joint Port Labor Relations Committee shall mutually consider appropriate.

I said, "Wow . . ."

"Do you know what this one sentence says?"

"That you can't drink on the job?"

"Actually, it covers a lot more than that. Who is in the position of power in this sentence?"

"The labor relations committee?"

"Exactly. And who are the people that are the target of this sentence?"

"All longshoremen?"

"Right again! Now all the parts between 'any longshoreman' and 'Joint Port Labor Relations Committee' list the things that this sentence is discussing. What are they?"

"Umm, let me see. Being drunk on the job? Disruption of normal harmony? Working in a hazardous manner?"

"Not bad. Physical assault is in there too. And what happens if a longshoreman does one of these things?"

"They can't drive a crane?"

"Nor a strad or even a forklift. This sentence pretty much puts a longshoreman on hard labor, so to speak. There is a lot more to analyze in this one long set of words, but you have the idea. I want you to break down each part that I assign you, and I want you to bring questions to our next meeting. I think you can see how much is in here and how hard it is to know exactly what is covered. That's where you will graduate from longshore worker to longshore contract expert. And you have to be an expert to put together the paper you need. Remember, the union has lawyers. You have to be able to cut through the chaff and get to the point, or they will bury you in it. Then you can put together a really good grievance."

"And this will make the union change?"

"Not directly. You're going to have to get all the players' attention. When some shipping company finds out there is a possible violation of federal law, then they will want to find ways to make sure this doesn't happen again. Ways like firing the worst offenders, mandatory training for workers, and fines and penalties to make everyone fall in line. Remember, CMA is there to keep things running smoothly. You're going to upset things until they come in line with their own contract to make things run like they say they should run. Without a penalty, men will do what men want to do. It's that simple. We're not very bright. You often need to hit us over the head like a stubborn mule to make sure you have our attention."

We laughed, which made my tension level drop a little. What Bill said made sense, and since I had no option of going backward, I had to proceed.

We opened up the contract over the next several weeks, and at times I felt a whole lot more like a lawyer than a longshoreman, but I certainly learned how much the contract had the ability to protect each union worker if it could be applied equally and fairly.

Bill also had me watch movies about union history and study union documents. One of the most important lessons was to document everything. Write it down, type it, make an audio record, do anything—but make a permanent record. It should have the date and time, the location, who was there, and what happened. You should have more than one copy, and you should keep those copies separate and safe. And never ever tell anyone that you are making a record. Someone that is your friend today can easily become your enemy tomorrow. It's unfortunate, but you can't trust anyone when you start documenting the wrongs in an organization."

I learned a lot from this process. Bill was 100 percent a union man, but he was also a man who saw things in black and white. He wanted the union to do the right thing, and he showed me how to put my grievance forward in the best way. We both wanted it to work.

We put together a script that pointed out where the union had broken its own laws, and it was a pretty powerful-looking tool. We put together a grievance and dropped it into the system. It made a splash.

A really big splash.

WORLD TRADE CENTER, PART I

My grievances resulted in a formal hearing. It was formal in that it was not at the union hall, but it was still run by the Joint Port Labor Relations Committee (JPLRC) and set up to make me look bad.

Our meeting was scheduled for the last part of December 1994. It still amazes me that from my first day at work in 1988 until now that the union refused to follow federal law and would force this meeting to happen.

The World Trade Center in Tacoma is probably the largest membership-based trade organization in the Pacific Northwest. The idea was to promote local business into the global marketplace. Exporters, importers, and service providers all meet here to work out inbound and outbound trade missions and contracts, so it was natural for the longshore union to use meeting rooms in the center.

We were scheduled for 9:00 a.m. on the twenty-ninth of the month. I got there five minutes early. By a quarter after nine, I was fuming. I told Ruben Hale I wanted this delay entered into the transcript of the meeting. By this time, I was pretty aware of the tools union management used to intimidate and demoralize anyone who stood up to them. I wasn't going to put up with it. A secretary in the office overheard me. It wasn't like I was trying to be subtle.

"There was another meeting scheduled for 9 a.m.," she said.

I almost yelled, "Why?"

"There is another meeting scheduled at ten as well," she mumbled.

I leaned over to Ruben. "I will not be rushed or intimidated."

At 10 a.m., Harold Thomas came out of the back room and told us to follow him.

"No!" I shouted.

Harold whined, "We only want to ask you some questions."

"And I want this delay in our meeting time read into the transcript. We were scheduled for nine, and now this meeting is an hour late. I won't put up with this!"

Harold left, stomping back into the room where he had come from.

Fifteen minutes later, we were finally escorted into the meeting room. It was not a very large room, and most of it was taken up by a large oblong table. I was put at one end, and Ruben took a chair next to me.

The JPLRC had gone to great lengths to ensure this meeting didn't have a chance of success. There were at least twenty people in the room, either sitting at the table or in chairs lined up against the walls and windows. We were here to discuss sexual discrimination, and I was the only female in the room. They had even managed to find a male court reporter.

There were a few men I recognized. Harry London, one of my worst tormentors, was sitting almost directly behind me. Dave Shindling, the current business agent and the person who should have functioned as a grievance mediator, was sitting at the table. Wilbur Stockton, a labor relations administrator, was sitting opposite me. Most of the other men were officials of the union or the Coastal Maritime Association.

One bright spot was Jeff Collins Jr., who was sitting by one of the windows. Lou Grebs was there, right next to him. Lou was a foreman at the port where the accident happened that caused my stepfather's death. We had always had a good working relationship, so I felt glad he was there. In an unfortunate twist of fate, Lou's son had been driving the strad that had collided with my stepfather's strad and caused his death.

The following are some of the high points from the meeting. These come from the court recording. What they do not indicate are the coughs, the yawns, and the laughs the men used to belittle me. They were trying their best to make the proceedings look unimportant.

Ralph Means, a labor relations administrator, opened the meeting. "This is a special hearing conducted by the Longshore Labor Relations Committee to investigate an alleged claim of discrimination, a violation of section 13. I'll read section 13 to refresh our memories.

> There shall be no discrimination in connection with any action subject to the terms of this agreement either in favor of or against any person because of membership or non-membership in the union, or absence thereof, or race, creed, color, sex, age, national origin, or religious or political beliefs.

"We received a letter from Linda Nyland, dated November 22, 1994. I'll read this for the record.

> To the Joint Port Labor Relations Committee, regarding a claim of sexual harassment/sex discrimination and a violation of the Equal Pay Act.

I am a Class "A" registered longshoreman and a member of the Tacoma local. I am submitting the following claim of sexual harassment, sexual discrimination, and violation of the Equal Pay Act.

My father, Robert Lizotte, was a registered longshoreman and a member of the union for 12 years. In November of 1987 he was killed in a straddle carrier accident, which occurred while he was employed by the Port of Tacoma.

My first contact with the union was with former Business Agent Barry Newsome when I requested registration under the permissive rule. Mr. Newsome was extremely rude and hostile. My request was denied because he said the union rule was only for sons. It took the intervention of the Coastal Maritime Association to initiate my registration process.

Since the beginning of my employment as a longshoreman, I have been the victim of sexual harassment and sex discrimination. Certainly not all but most of the sexual harassment has come from supervisory personnel. Their desire to bully and humiliate me is an abuse of their power, and their behavior has been rude, degrading, and unrelenting. Verbal harassment has been the most common, but I have also been the victim of physical abuse such as grabbing and touching.

The behavior toward myself has been and continues to be an indecent assault and irresponsible conduct, demonstrating disrespect and disregard for the rights of women.

The docks are sexist, male-oriented, and anti-female in atmosphere. Such an environment means or implies that tolerating an abusive, uncomfortable, and sexist workplace is part of the job.

The effect on my person has been increased anxiety, stress, depression, and loss of self-esteem. The sexual harassment undermines my self-confidence, impairs my health, and causes me to feel embarrassed, alone, and isolated.

Most strikingly, my payroll at Juniper Gate continues to be limited because of my gender. For approximately the last two years, I have been dispatched along with my male co-worker to checker and clerk jobs at Juniper and have been doing the same work for the same number of hours each day, but the man I work with has been receiving an hour of overtime each day and I have not. We are dispatched at 8 a.m. and work until 5 p.m. However, the foreman places the man on the payroll starting at 7 a.m., and that's what gives him an hour of overtime.

On October 14, 1994, I met with Dale Shindling, business agent for the union, and explained my grievance. He refused to represent me and told me I was on my own.

According to the Equal Pay Act, a woman doing the same work as a man is entitled to receive equal pay. To deny equal pay is a violation of federal law.

I request all sexual harassment and sexual discrimination stop immediately and that I am provided a working environment safe from verbal and physical harassment and abuse.

I also request back pay of $6,361.74, which is the amount of pay my male co-worker was given in overtime by the foreman, pay he was given for hours he did not work.

At this point, the men in the room started to play at being lawyers, although as far as I know, none of them were. They were all union management, foremen, or representatives of various longshore groups. Part of the strategy must have been to put any blame on whoever was not at the meeting, and that was the next statement from Ralph Means.

"I want to explain that this is a committee of employer and union representatives. However, there is no one here from the Port of Tacoma, and therefore we cannot represent them. The Port is not part of the Coastal Maritime Association, and so this committee has no authority to investigate or adjudicate claims against the Port."

Bene Laws, a union labor relations council member, spoke next. "I would like to establish for the record that Ms. Nyland has the opportunity in a claim of discrimination to have other representation if that representation is not an attorney and that Ms. Nyland has asked the union to not be involved."

I couldn't let that go. "I brought my grievances to the business agents many times. These men are supposed to support each worker and help us resolve any grievances. Each time I was told I was on my own. The union never reached out to me after any of my grievances."

Dale Shindling made a statement that made no sense to me. "You didn't answer the question that we asked you in regards to what statements you did make. I was referring to 'on your own' for anything over what the contract calls for."

How do you even respond to double-speak like that? It was obvious they had used the time before our meeting to come up with ways to try to confuse the issue. This kind of behavior was so detrimental to the union. Here they had a clear path to resolution that would cost very little, and it would bring them in line with federal employment law, rendering any other actions against the union mute. But they didn't want to do that.

At this point, I asked for us to go around the room and introduce ourselves, since I didn't know many of these men or what part of the union they represented. I discovered that some of the men were newly elected officers of the union who would not take over until after the new year.

Ruben spoke up. "I'd like to state for the record that we were scheduled for 9 a.m. and this meeting has started considerably later than that. We don't know why that was, but there seems to be either a lack of organization or an attempt at intimidation. We don't appreciate either one, and I want the record to reflect this.

"With that out of the way, pertaining to the representation issue raised by the union, clearly the longshore workers union is the designated collective bargaining agent, and Linda is a member of the union, and no one is allowed to change the legal representation issues this union is subject to. As far as the Port is concerned, I met with their general counsel and was instructed to process the grievance through the Coastal Maritime Association procedures. Linda was under the terms of the longshore contract while employed at Juniper Gate. The Port payrolls workers through the Coastal Maritime Association, and we are here to adjudicate her grievance in accordance with those contracts."

Bene Laws tried to wiggle out of the vice Ruben was tightening. "This hearing is to determine if Section 17.4 procedures under discrimination will be afforded in this instance. This hearing is not to determine the extent or investigate the grievance. Didn't you read the letter of 1985?"

"Not lately," Ruben said.

"Then I'll read it into the record. This is the labor relations letter of November 6, 1985, regarding discrimination grievances:

> Recently there have been a number of discrimination claims by individuals referred to this committee and subsequently to the coast arbitration officer which

in reality were regular or routine contract violation claims rather than discrimination claims in violation of Section 13 of the contract.

We call to your attention that the special grievance procedures set forth in Section 17.4 through 17.43 are applicable only on claims of discrimination in violation of section 13. These provisions extend to individuals certain grievance machinery rights not accorded to individuals in any other contractual claims which do not involve discrimination.

Therefore, it is very important that it be determined if, in fact, the claim is a proper grievance which falls under section 13. A mere claim of discrimination by the grievant is not sufficient. There must be a sound basis for classifying the grievance which appears to violate one of the acts prohibited by section 13.

The union management was trying to blow smoke and dispute the discrimination by a lot of fake posturing. It's also easy to see the union had been down this road before and didn't want to admit there was a problem or behave like adults.

Ruben Hale countered, "I would like to read from a letter dated August 14, 1992, and signed by Ralph Means, our labor relations administrator.

Discrimination on account of sex is a violation of Title VII of the Civil Rights Act of 1964 and a violation of the Coast Longshore and Clerk's Agreement. The EEOC has recently issued guidelines to define such discrimination. This includes the following: unwelcome sexual advances, requests for sexual favors and other verbal or physical conduct of a sexual nature when such conduct is made explicitly or implicitly a term or condition of employment, or is used as a basis for employment decisions or has the purpose or effect of interfering with work performance or of creating an otherwise offensive and hostile working environment.

The grievance machinery of the union is available to any employee who claims the former policies have been violated.

Ruben didn't give them a chance to counter. He turned to me. "Linda, are you an "A" registered union member?"

"Yes, I am."

"How long have you been a longshoreman?"

"Six and a half years."

"Have you ever experienced sexual harassment while working at the port?"

"Yes."

"Can you give us an example?"

I looked right at Harry London, one of my worst tormentors. "I was working on the docks. This was in the fall of '88. I walked away from the dog house shack where I was assigned and bent over to pick something up. Harry came up behind me, grabbed me by my hips, and pulled me into his groin."

Harry shouted, "NO!"

"And then he said to me, 'This is what you get for bending over.'"

"NO WAY! I NEVER DID ANYTHING LIKE THAT!"

"There was another time, in the fall of '92. I was leaving for the day and was in the parking lot. I was putting my key in the door of my car, and he came up behind me, grabbed me around the waist, swung me around, and said he wished he didn't have to go to work right now. The smell of alcohol on his breath was very strong. Someone else called to him and he left."

Harry was red-faced and livid. "You got any witnesses? I don't remember anything like that ever happening."

I said, "I don't feel Mr. London should be in judgment of me for sexual harassment he has done to me. I don't feel he should have a vote on my grievance, and more importantly, I don't think he should be in this room!"

Hugh Brooks, a Coastal Maritime representative said, "Linda, I think you are here to make your case and submit evidence, making any accusations you wish to make. We will then investigate your charges and answer you by letter."

WORLD TRADE CENTER, PART II

We'd been at it for a while and, it seemed things were getting heated, so a recess was called.

When we came back in, Dale Shindling spoke. "We discussed the issue during the break, and we have decided that Harry London will remain in this room and will be part of the process." There was little we could do to change that.

Ruben started up where we had left off. "Linda, you became registered in 1988?"

"Yes."

"Can you tell us what happened when you first phoned the union hall to find out about the permissive registration process?"

"Yes. My call was forwarded to the business agent, Barry Newsome. After asking how I should proceed under the permissive rule, he became violently angry. He told me the rule was for sons, not daughters, and he called me a 'f*cking whore.'

"He slammed the phone down, and frankly I was shocked. I had no idea anyone in a position of power in this day and age in America would act and speak like that. I persisted and called two more times, with the same result and even more cursing at me.

"It was then suggested I call the Coastal Maritime Association and also get in touch with the union's main office in San Francisco. There were individuals who helped me do what needed to be done, and I eventually was a registered "B" longshoreman."

At this point I recounted the incidents mentioned in the earlier chapters—the threats, sexual advances, spitting in my face, calling me names, and all the other ways they tried to wear me down. They were demanding names of those responsible, and since some of them were in the room, I became worried. "What system of safeguards are there to guarantee my safety? You're asking for names and dates, and so I'm getting worried about reprisals."

Hugh Brooks said, "Our policies prohibit retaliation."

I thought to myself, "Yes, and your policies prohibit exactly the kinds of discrimination and harassment we're talking about today, yet here we are." Then I said, "Do you have any system to move me to another port in case I feel my life is threatened?"

"Are you requesting a transfer? Because if you are . . ."

"No. I'm asking what protections or options are available to me."

"You can transfer to any port on the West Coast under our contract provisions."

"You don't get the point. There are lots of things in the contract, and it seems to me no one in this room or in the whole union has read any of it. We shouldn't be having this meeting because people should be abiding by the rules in the contract. And if there is a disagreement, then there should be a safe and sane grievance procedure that allows all parties to speak openly and calmly about what the needs are. Right now, we are all afraid to even try to use the provisions of the contract because it all funnels to the business agents who don't want to hear it. Yes, it's easier to ignore problems and hand them off to the next manager, but sooner or later, these things need to be resolved. Right now, I think I need to take another break."

Brooks agreed, and we had some time to cool down.

When we came back in, Ruben took the lead and steered the conversation to a less confrontational subject. "Linda, have you experienced sexual discrimination in the form of disparate pay while working as a longshoreman?"

"Yes. It happened at the Juniper Gate as I talked about earlier. My male co-worker got an hour overtime for at least two years, and I didn't, even though we worked the same hours."

"Can you tell me how this happened and how you came to know about it?"

"Yes. We both came into work around the same time. He and I would both be in the union hall waiting for pick so we could sign for our jobs. We always went out to the job site around 8 a.m., but the entry for his name always showed he was starting at 7 a.m. The payroll book is always open on the dispatch desk, so it's not a secret and it's not hard to see what hours you've been credited for, nor the workers you have been on shift with. It was blatantly obvious he had been given an extra hour of time-and-a-half pay and I was not, even though we worked exactly the same job in the exact same place during the exact same hours."

"Who put those hours on the payroll book?" Ruben asked.

"Whoever was foreman for the day."

"And it is part of a foreman's responsibility to ensure workers are on the job and getting paid for the work they are tasked to do? No more, no less?"

"That's right."

"What did you do to try and resolve this situation?"

"I talked several times with Stan Norris, the foreman. At first, he said he would look into it. I kept asking, and finally he said Mr. Burns would not give me the extra hour of overtime."

At this point, I could have brought up the whole "beating around the bush" incident. I felt like I couldn't. It would have created an uproar in the meeting. I think the men were expecting it, though, and if things progressed to a lawsuit, then I would ask my attorney to bring it up.

"What happened?"

"Nothing. It was never resolved."

Ruben stepped in to bring up some more about the pay issues. "While working for the Port of Tacoma at Juniper Gate, are you working under the terms and conditions of the Longshore and Clerk's contract?"

"Yes, I am."

"And your payroll is paid by Coastal Maritime Association?"

"Yes, it is."

Hugh Brooks, an employer representative spoke up. "Do you have any evidence to prove that?"

Ruben asked, "Which part?"

"The first part, the fact you were working under the terms and conditions of our longshore contract."

I said, "When I am dispatched out of our hall as a longshoreman, I dispatch under those conditions of the contract."

Brooks dismissively said, "That's your belief."

Ruben backed me up. "Are you dispatched by a joint dispatcher? By that I mean the same dispatcher that would dispatch you for any job you would take out of the hall as a member of the local union?"

"Yes, I am. All jobs come to us that way."

"Did anyone tell you when you were dispatched to any job that you were not covered by the Coastal Maritime Association contracts?"

"No."

"There is no difference in any job you take from any dispatcher in the union hall, is that correct?"

"Yes. No difference."

Ruben continued, "Finally I would like to submit for the record an executive board report of which the union has a copy. The executive board sent three members to do research in Seattle, Tacoma, and Portland, as it so states in this document, and they made some findings specifically related to Tacoma in the area of sexual harassment and dispatch problems. I am stating for the record that the union is well aware both internally and at the national level that they have problems which they have refused to address. That's why we're here today. We ask that you do a thorough investigation, that you deal with an open mind, and that you do the right thing."

Ruben said he wanted to question Jeff Collins Jr., the man who had been initially tasked with my first week of training and who had turned into an ally. Ruben asked, "Jeff, are you a registered longshoreman?"

"Yes. I've been a class "A" longshoreman for about three years now."

"And have you worked with Linda on the docks?"

"Yes, regularly. I do a lot of clerk jobs on the Juniper Gate, and Linda has been assigned there often."

"What's a typical day like as a clerk on that gate?"

"Normally one of us is inspecting trucks, while the other one is handling the paperwork—making sure everything is correct."

"Do you switch off these duties?"

"Yes, we do."

"So it's fair to say that both of you do the same job?"

"Yes. That's true."

"Are you dispatched for an 8 a.m. start?"

"Yes. Always."

"You were told to start work at 8 a.m., but on your payroll history, the foreman put you down for a 7 a.m. start?"

"Correct."

"And you were paid an extra hour every day?"

Jeff said, "It was the case until Linda sent in a letter asking why I and other workers were getting an hour of overtime and she wasn't. It stopped for everyone at that point."

"How did you know this?"

"The payroll sheets are not private. They're out on the desk, and anyone can take a look at them."

"Was it your understanding that when you were working these jobs when you were getting an hour of overtime that you were working under the terms and conditions of the longshore contract?"

"Yes."

"Were you and Linda dispatched by the same person for all jobs?"

"Yes."

"Did anyone ever tell you these jobs were not covered by the longshore contract?"

"I was never told nor was it implied. How else or who else would be paying us if not the Port under the longshore contract?"

"Is there anything on any of your paychecks stating that some of them were not covered by the longshore contract?"

"No, they all look the same."

Dale Shindling spoke up. "Jeff, if you get to the gate before 8 a.m., do you start work?"

"Sometimes. I feel guilty for getting an extra hour of overtime and not working for it, so if there are trucks ready, I sometimes jump in and get them processed."

Ruben asked, "Do you always do that if you arrive early?"

"Not always."

"If you don't show up early, do you still get paid for the extra hour?"

"Yes."

Ruben paused. "Jeff, when was the first time you got an extra hour of overtime?"

"It started on the very first day I came to work."

Ruben closed things up by saying, "I think that covers everything I wanted to explore."

That may have been all the men wanted to talk about, but to me they totally missed the point by not hearing me out. All these actions were never so much about a single man or group of supervisors as it was about the basic issues. They couldn't understand why it wasn't OK to treat women and minorities differently than they treated each other. They couldn't see that the problem was the systemic misogyny and prejudice rampant at the union and management level.

The meeting ended with an agreement from the men in the room that they would "let me know" what they decided and that I would get a transcript of the meeting.

CHANGE OF PLANS

All the details of the hearing made it back to the dock before I did.

Jerry Newsome was one of the people I had mentioned in the deposition. He was one of the men who made continual comments about my "jugs." His response was immediate and dangerous. "I'm going to kill the f*cking bitch! I'll make sure she never walks again!"

He wasn't the only one. Some of the threats were delivered face to face. Most were behind my back.

"You need to watch your back 'cause you never know when a can is going to fall from the crane."

"Next time a forklift might not miss you."

"She better not work with me because I won't watch her back."

"I'm gonna stomp her face into the ground."

"I'm gonna bomb her house."

"Does anyone know how to make a Molotov cocktail? I think we need to make a midnight delivery."

"I'm going to run her over like a seagull."

If you don't live in the Northwest, you probably don't know about seagulls. They are large birds that have learned where there are humans there is often food. They are also large enough that they don't always fly off when danger approaches but, rather, waddle away. Longshoremen at Tacoma routinely ran over seagulls, partly because they wouldn't move and partly out of disgust.

I was really concerned for my safety. One day, one of the men who supported me offered me a gun, so I went out and got my concealed weapons permit.

The rest of the people stayed away from me for two reasons. One, those who knew they were guilty were afraid of being mentioned in any further actions I might take. Two, those who quietly agreed with me didn't want to say or do anything to support me as they would be guilty by association.

I was riding in a pickup, and we were making our way down a line of railway cars. My job was to hop out and install the dogs (locks) to hold the container to the railcar. We always had the communications radio on, and as I got back in from making an installation, I heard, "Don't say anything to her; you might get brought up on charges."

While I certainly expected verbal and physical violence, I knew whom to keep away from, and my silent supporters kept me separated from those who would hurt me. I was extremely lucky. The only instances were times when I was backed up into a corner and screamed at. The rest of the time those that hated me acted like I didn't exist and looked right through me. I was being ostracized. I could live with that.

A few weeks later, I got a letter in the mail, and it said my grievance was denied.

> The Joint Labor Relations Committee agreed that your pay claims while working at the Port are not

properly before the JPLRC, as the Port is not a member of the Coastal Maritime Association, and therefore, the JPLRC has no jurisdiction or control over the Port. Individuals working at the Port do not work under the terms and conditions of the Longshore and Clerk's Contract Agreement.

The Committee further agreed that regarding your claim of sexual harassment/discrimination that the instances and information described took place over six months ago and took place in the workplace of a non-CMA member which are not under the jurisdiction of the JPLRC.

So here was their way out. There was no way to bring a grievance before the committee within six months as they delayed and postponed all actions until well after any six-month time period. The Port was nothing more than a government framework to specify where ships could come in and load or unload. They didn't hire or assign any longshoremen, so they were shifting blame to someone who had no authority. Considering their behavior all along, I shouldn't have been surprised.

The only way to try to get someone to listen was to put in a grievance every time there was discrimination or harassment. That would perhaps meet the six-months' time limit, but it would make whoever did that look like a troublemaker. That was not feasible.

Things changed at work, though. Back on the very first day I worked with Gary Burican, he was staring at, commenting on, and fascinated by my breasts. It was childish, and how he could think his comments were appropriate is beyond belief. To hear how his comments changed from day one until now shows the mentality of too many of the longshoremen. This is how he started out:

"Oh, your boobs are so bouncy today. Are you wearing a bra?"

The next day it was, "I really love your ass, but your boobs are the best part of you!"

The day after that it was, "I just love cold days because it makes your nipples show through your shirt."

It was like this every day that I worked with him. I tried hard to avoid him, but even if I ran into him in the hall, it was boob comments all over again. At the stop where we would get on the bus to be taken to the ship, he would stand where he could watch me so he could comment on how my breasts bounced. It was continual, over and over, and he seemed to think there was nothing wrong with it. Later after my grievance over pay hours, a rumor started that I was going to cause all the workers who were getting an unearned hour of overtime to lose it.

This guy, who used to make sexual comments to me, told Jeff I better not be on any jobs he was working on because I might get hurt. So he went from sexual harassment for his own pleasure to threatening me with bodily harm.

I was pretty dejected, but Bill told me all it did was change how we would now play the game. He told me what I needed to do to take things to the next level.

"From now on, everything you send to them goes by certified letter. That creates a paper trail, and there's none of this 'we never got it' bull." He told me to include the union headquarters in San Francisco in my letters and to send everything certified mail.

An unforeseen result was that all the union responses were also sent certified mail, so now I had a documented record back and forth of "she said, they said."

I made a copy of everything and kept those safe. Now there was always one copy going to Tacoma, one to San Francisco, and one to my personal files. If I had known better, I would have been doing that all along.

Since my grievance was denied, Bill told me to send copies of all my documentation to the coast office in San Francisco. They selected an arbitrator to look at my case.

The arbitrator looked at all the documentation and decided there was nothing to be done to resolve the situation. This allowed me to legally go outside the union to try to resolve the problems.

Both Bill and Ruben said the next move was a lawsuit. So I found an attorney. I went to the law library in the County-City Building and found a reference showing attorneys and their specialties. I found a woman who had written a book on sexual harassment and thought she might be a good choice to represent me. I signed a contract with her in early 1995. She did come to some of the union meetings with me, but after a while, it seemed to me she was getting too friendly with some of the union men rather than collecting information to support me.

Around that same time, I felt like I needed help from a counselor. All the stress of constant harassment was wearing on me. I found one I thought would help. She didn't. Our first meeting was our last.

"Linda, how can I help you?"

"I'm stressed from work."

"What kind of stress?"

"There is a lot of sexual harassment, name calling, discrimination when it comes to assignment of jobs, just about anything you can imagine."

"Where do you work?"

"I'm a longshoreman on the Tacoma docks."

There was a long period of silence.

"I can't help you."

Now it was my turn to go silent.

"What do you mean? Why not?"

"Linda, I have other clients who are longshoremen. I know what they are capable of. I can't take a chance one of them would find out you are also a client of mine. I can't take a chance of having my business burned down or some other kind of personal vendetta against me. I'm really sorry, but the personal and professional risk is too great. I can't have you as a client."

I left completely dejected. I'd never known anyone turned down by a counselor! In my mind, they were kind of like doctors; they should help you, no matter what. A counselor had refused to help me when I needed it most. It really stung. I went home numb and not really sure what to do.

Meanwhile, I continued to work with my lawyer. I took her the notes I had been collecting over the years in the hope she would help me. I still thought she was getting a little too familiar with some of the longshoremen, and she even asked me if I was making too much out of the incidents I had reported to her. But I also still thought she was basically on my side. After all, she was my lawyer.

The notes I took her were not all the records I had ever collected or written; others I had stored in the garage where I thought they would be safe in their plastic bins. But I hadn't counted on the critters. I lived next to a wooded area. At some point 120 acres of trees were cleared. All the woodrats suddenly felt quite homeless. Some of them invaded the garage and found my papers. They ate through the plastic of the containers and then made really nice (in a rat's mind) beds inside. I had to throw out a lot of paper. It wasn't salvageable. and I wouldn't have wanted to be taping rat-chewed pages back together anyway.

Things kept humming along, and then I got a call from her office asking if I could come up. Finally something was going to happen with my case!

I took the next day off, and when I arrived in her office, I was shown into a meeting room. My box of notes was brought in and put on the table. She came in and said, "We are returning all of your documentation. There is nothing we can do for you."

Once again, I was dropped by someone who I thought was going to help me. I don't know how I got that huge box down to my car by myself, but I did. It's a miracle I made it home without getting in an accident. I was crying so hard I could barely see the lines on the road, but somehow I did it. My daughter was at the babysitters, so I collapsed into my rocking chair. I was totally crushed. There was nothing else to do. As I always do when I feel backed into a corner, I said a little prayer. "Lord, I don't know if I'm doing the right thing or if I'm on the right path. I give my future to you. If this is what I'm supposed to be doing, show me the way. Tell me what you want of me." In less than an hour, the phone woke me up. It was one of my female co-workers.

"Hey, Linda! I heard you got an attorney and you have a lot of documents for your case."

"Yes, I do have documents."

"You sound really down. Are you OK?"

I guess my pain—although not the source—of being dumped by my attorney must have been obvious. "I just got home from my attorney in Seattle. She dumped me. No reason. She just told me she couldn't represent me."

"That seems like a really strange thing for her to do." She paused for a minute and then said, "I know. You should come over and talk to our lawyers."

There were three women working with a local lawyer. These three had a case against the union for not promoting them past casual status.

"OK. I'll call them. Let me have their number." I talked to them, and they readily set up an appointment for me. The next day, I went to see their lawyer. I didn't think anything would come out of it, and I was leery of getting my hopes up, but it felt like the hand of God guiding me once again.

"Thank you, Linda, for coming to see us and for talking about the possibility of using your notes to support your co-workers' suits."

"You're welcome. I started taking notes from the very first day. It was such an out-of-the-ordinary working environment that I didn't think anyone would believe me if I didn't have notes. It was literally like traveling back in time to the 1950s. It still is. It's bizarre."

They had my box brought in, and we went through some of the papers. It didn't take long for the attorneys to come up with a proposal. "Would you let us represent you?"

"I don't want to join the other three women. I support what they're doing, but the two situations are completely different. They came in as casual workers and are being denied promotion to "B" registered status. I came into the union on the very first day as a registered "B" worker under the hardship rule. My stepfather was killed in an accident on the docks. It was a fight, but they finally had to let me in. My lawsuit needs to be about job discrimination, sexual harassment, and equal pay.

"That sounds fine. We could proceed with two separate lawsuits. If you would allow us to use your notes in support of both actions, I feel confident we could win. They do have a good case, but with your notes to back them up, it makes everything much stronger."

Now I was sure the hand of God had put this together. "This sounds good to me. Let's do it!" I signed a contract with them, and the next time we got together, I found a lot of my notes were missing. The items that were missing all pertained to certain people—like port commissioners and other high-ranking union bosses. I couldn't prove it, but it looked like my previous attorney had pulled out the documents that could hurt individual men at the top of the union. It was one of the most disgusting things I had ever known a lawyer to do, certainly illegal, but on the other hand, I should have had copies of everything. It was a hard lesson. All through this process, I'd made notes not knowing where it would lead me. I didn't have a lot of extra money, and certainly not enough for a copier. This was back in the nineties. I couldn't have been at a library making copies for hours, and I certainly wasn't going to drop off all my notes at some photocopy business and trust they wouldn't read them. You never know who is related to someone in the union, and I just couldn't take that chance. So some powerful people were let off the hook because papers were lost . . . or stolen.

My new attorneys were not fazed at all. "Linda, there is more than enough here to show how they have treated minorities and women. This material represents you and all those on the docks they have discriminated against."

This law firm also had contacts that were counselors and doctors who were not afraid of the union and that would testify in court. Now finally I had a counselor I could talk to about how the pressure at work was affecting me and ways I could work through those issues. There were doctors ready to prescribe anything I needed to get well again.

Once again, the hand of God reached out and helped me stand up, strong and able. It was a miracle how help came and how it always came just in time. I tried to do all I could by myself. I've never been one to sit back and let someone else do everything for me, and to be honest, I don't think God would have helped me if I'd lived my life like that. But He was always there for me, every single time I needed Him.

For instance, I needed to pay Ruben Hale for helping me. Ruben was being really supportive and told me I could pay him when I got the money. But I know if I wouldn't pay a bill today, it would slide to the bottom of the pile and get lost. So I always pay my bills promptly, and those people who are doing so much to help me always go to the top of my list.

The bill was $550. I'd been trying for weeks to find the money, but it was all I could do just to pay my regular monthly bills. Five hundred was an enormous sum at that point in my life. The bill was weighing on me, even though Ruben was not pressuring me. So I asked for help from the one I knew could help. "Lord, I don't know how I can pay this bill, so I'm putting it in your hands. Show me what I need to do."

The very next day, I got a child support payment for $550! Child support had always been hit or miss, and monthly payments had never been that much, but there it was! You can call it what you like, but I called it a miracle. I paid Ruben, and my stress level went down. Thank you, Lord!

It took about a year for our lawsuits to move through the system.

When word got out I was taking the union to court and suing them, the rumors (what we call fake news today) started flying.

"Hey, Linda! I heard you sued the chemical company you used to work at and put them out of business. Didn't get enough money from that? Gotta take down the union too? How much did you get when you sued them? Millions? You sure are a greedy bitch! I heard you don't even pay union dues."

That last bit—actually, of course, all of it—was completely false. I paid dues just like everyone else.

"What does it feel like to put men out of work who are trying to make a living to support their families?"

"You're disgusting, you know that?"

"Accidents can happen. At any time, anywhere."

In fact I had never sued anyone or any business before the problems with the longshore union. I didn't even know how to go about it. I had a good relationship with everyone at the chemical company. I had maxed out my wage level there, and like these "honest men," I needed to support my daughter in the best way possible. I would never have sued the union if they had lived by federal law.

IF HE KNEW ME, WOULD HE LIKE ME?

The kind of abuse I had been putting up with spilled over into my personal life. My marriage had long ago become a casualty. It added to the feeling the world was never going to work for me in the way I wanted it to. I was definitely lonely. However, I stopped dating completely. My daughter was my world, and I refused to do anything that would put her in any kind of jeopardy or take time away from her.

My emotions told me I needed someone in my life, but on the on the other hand, I couldn't do it. I took some time to put my feelings down on paper. Here's what I wrote:

> I look into people's eyes at work and what I get back is sometimes hate and sometimes disgust. Some look right through me; some walk away. I feel very alone, even though I'm in the middle of so many people.
>
> Only with the help of God and the few good people He has sent to me can I make it through this. I have a beautiful daughter who loves me, no matter what. Her

big beautiful brown eyes look at me with love, and it opens my heart.

The negative energy builds inside of me, and I have to vent to let it out. I have to come home and isolate in the yard by beating a weed senseless.

This is all so hard on my daughter because I come home frustrated. I tell her to come straight home, get the dogs in the house, lock the doors, and stay inside. She's all alone, and I still have deep-seated fears about things that can happen. I have to keep her safe when I'm not there. It's hard on her, and none of it is her fault. It tears me up.

I have had so many years of being alone. My family says they support me, but how? With words? I need more.

Hey, family! Did you know someone is stealing my garbage? That's really disgusting, but it shows me how hard my enemies are working to take me down. It makes me all the more careful about what I throw away.

All this stress is turning my heart to stone. My stress level on a scale of one to ten is probably at twelve, and still I have to go to the hall and face all the trouble just to make a living. I've had to work hard all my life, even from childhood. This one job can take me out of poverty so I can break the chain that has tried to keep me down all my life. I have to do this for myself and for my daughter. I can't give up. I won't give up.

Professional help? Ha! The shrink says I should quit. My doc says I could quit. Counselors are too afraid of the union to even let me into their office. So if I quit, then what? Are you going to pay my bills, Doc? I didn't think so. So give me some advice that's actually worth your inflated hourly rate and your fancy degree. You can't, can you? Because the truth is the only way out is through the pain and the abuse.

College? Yeah, right! Who's going to support us for those four years—or more? And then if I'm lucky, really lucky, I might get a good job, but I'll be paying back student loans for the rest of my life. Somehow, I don't see that as a financially viable alternative. Going into debt to make the same money you would have with a high school diploma isn't realistic. I've seen a lot of my friends spend all that money to get a degree and a good job, and then some corporate ass sends their job overseas. No, thanks. I've found the only solution; I just need some help eliminating the human waste from this particular cesspool.

Friends and family say the same thing. Quit.

Let's be realistic. Should I drop back into the poverty that keeps trying to suck me back into the mire? I will not. Even though this is the hardest thing I have ever done in my life, I will not quit. I will come out at the other side a winner, and those who told me to quit will have to sit back and learn from me. That's where the best advice comes from anyway, from hard, cold personal experience, and I have that in spades.

When I am approached outside of work, I very, very seldom admit I am a longshoreman. It's not what anyone wants to hear. It's a job a lot of them wouldn't have the physical or mental strength to do. They wouldn't be able to put up with the bull long enough to rise up in spite of it all. So, no, I don't tell them. If you can't be open with someone you want to get to know, why bother at all? That's not me.

When I'm in a restaurant and I see another longshoreman, I usually look away. Most of them glare at me anyway. I can't get comfortable seeing a longshoreman away from work. Why would I? When you get death threats from your co-workers, it puts you on guard against everyone. The face smiling at me right now might be the one who sends a .357 bullet my way. Some of these men will do absolutely anything for money. Money buys them women, booze, and drugs, and there are addicts of all three working the docks. They need the fix more than they need their self-respect. Besides, I hit the big boys in their pocketbooks, and it's hard to let sleeping dogs lie.

And now I have started something. Something small, but it is happening. I have been a tiny pebble dropped onto the surface of a very large lake. I've made a little splash, but the ripples are spreading out, and others like me are seeing just what is possible.

END RUN

About two months before our case was due to be heard in court, the union must have realized this was going to happen, no matter what it did. So it made some last-minute moves to try to get out of the way of the disaster about to run it over.

It promoted a woman to supervisor, which was a rare occurrence. "See, we're not against women! We made one a boss!"

She was deserving of the promotion, but I had to wonder if she would have been promoted if the lawsuit hadn't forced the union to look for some way to appear blameless.

An earlier promotion of a woman had happened years before because of a grievance. This woman and a black man put in papers after futile attempts to be promoted to clerk positions. They had the qualifications and the seniority, but it wasn't happening. I never knew many of the details, and it would have been helpful to me. I did know that these two were a rare occurrence that wasn't repeated until our lawsuits.

The second action looked like a really dumb idea at first. The union set up a meeting with all the female longshore union members and proposed a class action suit against the union, using its own lawyers.

Yes, you read that right.

The union was going to sue itself in a class action by its own members and have its own lawyers perform the lawsuit!

Women who were wives and girlfriends of longshoremen seemed in favor of the idea. It's not hard to realize how much stress they would have been under at home if they hadn't been. But none of the other women agreed. The lawyers proposed they meet later to talk some more.

The beauty of this idea (for the union) was that it is almost impossible to have two active class action suits against the same defendant by the same set of plaintiffs. Once the class action was in place, the union would have likely tried to force the four of us to be absorbed into its class action. Then the union would have had its own lawyers try the case, and of course, any remedies would have been determined by the union through its attorneys.

It was a way to take over and try to end up with a settlement that would be a mere slap on the wrist for the union. Then it could go back to its old way of operation. If anyone complained, it could say, "Why are you complaining? You sued us and won! Are you just out for the money?"

Word of the evening meeting traveled quickly, and pretty soon I got a call from Jan. The four of us who had a lawsuit in the works thought this potential class action was something our own lawyers should be aware of. The next morning, we four were in their office, and that's how the end run the union attempted ended up with our own lawyers starting a class action themselves. All the female longshoremen were invited, and this time almost every one of them thought this was a really good idea.

Now the union had three lawsuits: mine, the three women who were being denied promotions, and almost every other female worker in the union! (The four of us were not included in the class action suit.) The men should have realized—women aren't stupid!

At this point, since one set of lawyers (ours) was pursuing three lawsuits against the same union, all the documentation the four of us had put together was now available to support the class action.

The union screamed. It felt betrayed and hurt. But this was just our attempt to get the union to operate how it was supposed to work. Unions are in place to make sure the workplace is safe and fair. The women of the union were banding together for their own good just like the original unions, and if things had been working correctly all along, none of this would have happened. We were only asking for the union to abide by the contract and federal law. It should have never come to this.

Women who had been unable or too afraid to say anything now flocked to the class action. Even though I had been fighting almost totally alone for years, I could understand why other women had not voiced their support before now. I can't tell you the full extent of the damage I suffered over all those years. The isolation, fear, stress, and harassment tore me apart and left deep emotional scars. I was raised tough, but all this stress was almost more than I could bear. I could completely understand why other women might not have felt strong enough to stand with me until there was the protection of lawyers.

With all this legal action, a minor but important point surfaced out of the contract. As mentioned earlier, the contract was hard to understand, so it is not surprising no one had discovered this gem until now, but hidden in all the legalese was a section about promotions. It said if you had worked for five years as a "B" and had not had any problems, then you should be promoted to "A" status. That was a very big deal, and now the union had to address this issue because it flew through the grapevine like wildfire. From a financial standpoint, it didn't cost the union anything. You got the same money for a job, no matter if you were "B" or "A" status. The difference between the two was in the job the worker got for the day. As an "A," you had more control over the types of jobs you picked for the day, rather than take what the dispatcher forced you to do. All the work had to be done, so letting workers do the kinds of jobs they enjoyed made the working environment better.

This took power away from the union bosses because now there was one less carrot to force workers to bend to their will. It was a lot harder, in fact almost impossible, to fire an "A" worker. "B" workers were much more vulnerable.

"A" and "B" were nothing more than a grade level that said you had worked the docks for five years, you had done a good job, and you were now deserving of better treatment. There was no good reason for the union to oppose this, especially since it was in the contract, but it screamed like the Devil himself had grabbed them hard in the softest of places.

NOVEMBER 25, 1996: US DISTRICT COURT, TACOMA, WASHINGTON

Four women and a class action of female longshoremen sued the union. It certainly didn't have to be this way. As I said before, I still believe in unions and didn't want do anything to hurt the union. I truly believe what we did was make it better and bring Tacoma into alignment with the other longshore unions along the west coast.

We met on November 25, 1996, to give our depositions, which in civil suits is often a first step. The attorney for the union was Lawrence Dupre. He tried to bring up the same idea as the guys at the World Trade Center meeting did—that all the terminals paid longshore workers separately, so none of them were responsible for what another did.

Then we went over the same pay and sex discrimination issues that had been brought up before.

Lawrence DuPre said, "Who was the employer on this

occasion?"

I replied, "I don't know. I pay attention to where I am assigned to work and what work I am responsible to complete. I don't keep track of who's the ultimate employer because I am being dispatched as a longshoreman so I'm going to get paid as a longshoreman."

"But if you're dispatched, let's say work for Carl's Stevedoring, you don't expect Ralph's Stevedoring to make out your check, do you? Don't you ever look at your check to see who's actually paying you?"

"They're all paying Coastal Maritime to pay me, so I don't worry about it."

"If you have a shortage—a problem with your check—who do you talk to about fixing it?"

"The pay clerk in the office. I've never had any problems that can't be fixed at that level."

DuPre switched to another subject. "Let's talk about the bathroom issue. What was the issue there?"

"Before 1990, most work places on the waterfront had only one bathroom—the men's room. There were usually one or two stalls, and normally only one had a door. These were next to urinals where the men would stand. I would ask someone to watch the door so I could go in, or I would wait until break was almost over. Without fail, men would barge into the bathroom as soon as they saw me go in. It was always the same, 'I've got it out, Linda. Wanna see? Wanna come look?' It was absolutely degrading."

"Did you complain?"

"Yes, and the answer was always the same. Quit if you don't like it."

"Who said that?"

"I don't have specific names. It happened every time I complained. I complained to foremen, dispatchers, people in the office, everyone. They all told me to quit if I didn't like it."

"Do you remember the foreman's name?"

"No. You could look it up in the logs, but at this point I don't remember."

"Did you complain to any other union officials?"

"They'd just laugh at me."

"My question was, did you complain to any union official?"

"After hearing women don't belong here and how I should just get off the beach, you know, you just get beaten down."

"Could I have an answer to the question?"

One of the other lawyers for the union said, "I'll move to strike the answer as unresponsive."

DuPre pressed the point. "I need a yes or no answer to the question."

I paused. "No."

He shifted to another issue. "You have an entry here that talks about a problem at one of the piers. Can you tell us about that?"

"Yes. I was driving a forklift, and the foreman came up to me and started screaming at me. 'We'd be done by now if it wasn't for you! You're driving too slow! We need to get this ship loaded.' But in fact, the hook to lift the cargo into the ship was broken. We couldn't get anything in or out."

"Did you explain that to him?"

"I couldn't get a word in edgewise. He was yelling, 'Women have no place here on the docks! You're useless!'"

"So what did you do?"

"Nothing. There was nothing I could do. Our only option was to wait for the hook to be replaced."

"You didn't bring this to anyone else's attention?"

"Who? My foreman? He was the one yelling! The shop steward? We don't have them."

"I'll move to strike the answer as unresponsive." DuPre then took up another position. "Turn to page 2931. These were probably notes you took some time after the fact?"

"No. I wrote this on the day it happened."

"Good. Tell us what happened on this day."

"A male and female longshoreman were standing outside the checker shack with me. It was slow, and they were pretty good friends. They started grabbing at each other in a sexual way. And then out of the blue, she says, 'Why don't you grab Linda for a while?' She walked out, and the man walked over to me and put his hands about four inches away from my breasts and said, 'How do they feel when they're full of milk?'"

"What did you do?"

"I told him if he touched me, I was going to call the police, then go to the union hall, and make a formal complaint."

"How did he respond?"

"He stared at me for a couple of minutes, and then he walked away."

"Did you talk to the female longshoreman about this? Because it seems like she instigated this and she was really the one responsible."

"No."

"Did you follow through with any of the things you told the man you were going to do?"

"No."

"You didn't make any kind of report or complaint?"

"No."

"Why not?"

"I was embarrassed and upset."

"Did you confide in any of the other female longshoremen?"

"No."

"That seems strange. Don't you have friends in the group?"

"I am friendly, but you can't trust anyone on the docks. There is only one person in the whole union I trust, and that's Jeff Collins Jr."

"OK. Let's look at page 2934. Can you tell us what happened

on that day?"

"I was working as a checker at one of the gates. The first thing in the morning, the boss and two "A" men started drinking on the job."

"Who were they?"

"I don't remember."

"If you remember later, please let us know. Then what happened?"

"One of them started asking about my love life and told me I needed a real man. He also said I probably like it both ways, meaning with men and women. Then he started telling me about his experiences with lots of women."

"And how did you respond?"

"I told him I was saving myself for Bill Gates."

A lot of people in the room chuckled.

"How long did this episode last?"

"All day. They were drinking and joking around all day."

"Did you make a complaint?"

"How could I? Who would I complain to? This was normal behavior for a lot of the workers on the docks."

"Yes or no."

"No."

"Let's talk now about the pornographic pictures in the work area. This was in one of the warehouses?"

"It was at one end, in the break room."

"And what was there that you found offensive?"

"The whole break room was covered in centerfolds, from floor to ceiling. There was one I found more offensive than the others. It was a woman on all fours, with her back to the camera and she was nude. Someone had written on it 'Yum, yum, strawberries!' I tried to ignore all of it, but it got to be too much. I stood up and told the guys in there that I was going to start taking them down and if anyone claimed them, they could have them. No one did."

"Did that solve the problem?"

"No. For at least two weeks, I ended up working alone. They gave me really heavy work to do, and normally there would be two longshoremen assigned together. After the incident with the porn, no one would work with me. The second longshoreman would walk out of the container or warehouse, and I'd have to do it all myself."

"What did you do?"

"I just did the best I could."

"You didn't make a complaint?"

"The more I complained, the harder things got for me, so no."

DuPre looked at his notes. "Let's go now to your notes about computer training. What kind of training was this?"

"Supervisory work on the computers related to clerk duties."

"What was the issue here?"

"I took the training and passed, but it wasn't entered on my Coastal Maritime longshoreman card."

"Maybe it wasn't entered on anyone's card."

"No. I've seen other cards of longshoremen who took the course, and it's stamped on the back of theirs."

"What did you infer from the fact that your card was not annotated?"

"Terry Nuell ran the computer training. He'd been asking to come over to my house or for me to go out with him for weeks. I always said no, but he wouldn't give up. I always felt like this was in retaliation for that."

"OK. I'd like to look at this entry about a discussion which included your daughter. Can you tell us about that?"

"Yes. We were sitting around on break, and someone asked about my daughter and what she liked to do. I said she really loves to dance and she is taking ballet lessons. The guys started joking about how she would grow up to dance at a strip joint. I yelled at them that she is only four years old and that this is family—'You should show some respect.' They laughed. That's another reason why I don't have friends on the docks. You can't have a normal friendly conversation without someone turning it into something dirty."

The lawyer must have seen that as a dead end, so he changed the subject. "I see here there was a problem with training. What was that about?"

"I have been trying to get training on cranes. I got my name on two crane training lists, and in both cases the union lost them. I managed to get on a strad training list, and on the very first day, the trainer said I would not pass, and of course I didn't. He was the one who had the final say. Last year I got on another strad list, and this time I easily passed. Different trainer, different outlook, and different outcome."

"When did the trainer tell you that you wouldn't pass the first strad training?"

"The first day, as we were getting training materials."

"It says here in your records that you quit."

"I didn't quit. I stayed in the training and came back for the second and third day."

"Why did you do that?"

"I thought maybe he would change his mind when he realized how motivated I was."

"Did he give a reason why you would fail?"

"He said he didn't want women working as strad drivers, and he said that to all the women who have tried to take the training."

"Was there any action taken by Coastal Maritime at all?"

"Yes. They conducted a private, internal investigation."

"When was this?"

"In November 1994, after my grievance."

"Who conducted this investigation?"

"An outside attorney."

"What was her name?"

"I don't remember."

"Did you personally meet with her?"

"Yes, for about four hours."

"Was anyone else present?"

"No, just her and I."

"Did you cover both the sexual harassment and the pay issues?"

"Yes, we did."

"What was the attorney's assessment of the case?"

"She seemed sad that all this had occurred, but other than that, she didn't say much."

"Did she tell you what might be done about these issues?"

"No. I did ask her if I could have a copy of her report and could I give that to my personal attorney. She said yes, that would be fine."

"What did you do with your copy?"

"I was never given one. It all went away, and nothing ever came of it."

We continued like this with the issues you read in the earlier chapters.

Eventually the deposition was over, and now we waited for the next step.

JUDGMENT DAY

After we were done, it was up to the court to make a decision. We came back the next day, and were there at eight that morning. At first, I was excited and anxious to finally see the end of the process. The day wore on as we waited for the decision. We went to lunch and came back. Still no word. Around nine that night, someone brought in pizza. I was ready to pack it in and leave, but the opposition said if any of us left, the settlement was not going to happen. The waiting was almost as hard as all that had come before. I had worn a dress to the court with the intention of looking professional and business like. Eventually I was so tired that I had to lie down on the carpet, dress and all. We were all exhausted.

Once again union management was testing me, trying to pressure me to quit, trying to get me to settle for something less. I refused. All I had ever wanted was to be heard. At any point in this whole process, the union could have lived up to what was written in the union contract. It could have agreed to work by federal law. It could have treated all workers as equal human beings. But it didn't want to do that. In the end, it cost the union dearly. Around one in the morning, we finally had a settlement. We had won. It was a victory for all workers on the docks.

The way I was treated changed. Now, instead of sexual remarks about going to a motel or "let me feel your jugs," the comments changed to "She's dead. Don't let me get close to her, or she's going to have an accident."

There was a small cadre of men who were quietly on my side. They couldn't come out and say it, but they were there listening for the threats, and when they had a chance, they told who said it and what kind of threat it was. They kept me alive. I completely understood why they couldn't say anything out loud. I had been branded a traitor to the union, even though I was trying to make it better. I was being threatened, and if they stood up for me, then they would also be at risk. This way was better. The four of us women were the targets, but we had a good portion of the dock workers watching our backs.

The threats must have been seen by the union management as a liability. After all, the lawsuit and the union's actions had been published in the news. If the star witness ended up dead, well, that would really put the union under a microscope. So it found a way to keep me a little safer. I became a registered clerk.

On most docks, there are three unions: foremen, longshoremen, and clerks. Tacoma was an exception as there were only two unions: foremen and a combined longshoremen and clerks union. This is what made us a dual charter local. There were a certain number of clerk positions, but they were never filled to capacity. That way any longshoreman could be temporarily assigned as a clerk, but it didn't work the other way around.

There was another facet of the clerk job that probably made me put off taking these jobs before this. The business agent could assign anyone to clerk duties, and this was often done to reward someone. It was inside and not physical. In fact, most of the longshore workers called it the Sick, Lame, and Lazy List when someone got assigned as a clerk. The macho side of the men wanted to be out there physically working, instead of sitting inside doing "women's" work.

Clerks were on a different pay scale as well, so I ended up with a raise. Having a combined longshore and clerk union meant management could put me into clerk jobs with nothing more than making the assignment.

Clerk jobs were mostly about the accounting and tracking of materials. You might be at a gate, recording the number painted on a container as a semi delivered it. You could also work in a warehouse where pallets of material were shuffled into new groups for delivery to other states and destinations. The manifests had to be checked and weights, dimensions, and destinations had to be recorded. Clerks didn't do much physical labor. It was mostly mental. And it took me off the docks where tons of material could "accidently" drop on my head. I was always inside with other people around, so it made me safer. Not completely safe, but much more so than if I'd been working outside.

There was another big benefit. Clerks did not come in for "pick" where a dispatcher handed out the best jobs to his cronies. Clerks got called at home with a list of jobs for the day, and for the most part, you could select the one you wanted. The call came an hour or so before work started because the clerk needed to be in position to accept the first shipments.

Another benefit was since there were few clerks, their names and the hours they'd worked were posted on a board in the union hall. Jobs were given out based on hours worked, so there was no way to deny someone work because their hours were posted on the wall for all to see. There were a couple of dispatchers who tried to deny me work, but I confronted them with the evidence written on their own work board, and so that stopped pretty quickly.

There were other changes that didn't benefit me, but these things made the union more fair for all citizens. Before the lawsuit, you had to be invited by a union member to come in and apply for work. Now anyone could apply, and the union had to accept workers sent over by the Washington State unemployment office.

In cases where a worker didn't make the grade, it became my fault in the eyes of the old guard. "You're the one that caused us to have to take people from unemployment lines! It's your fault when they don't work out! You train them!"

Slowly, the numbers of women and minorities working and getting promoted started to come up to what existed outside the union. All kinds of minorities started working on the docks.

Even with the changes, I was still very paranoid and defensive. I was out on the docks when a man I hadn't seen before came up to me.

"Are you Linda?"

I was instantly on guard. "Yes. What do you want?"

"Are you the woman who started the lawsuit?" he growled.

Now I was really tense. "Yes."

"I want to thank you. Can I shake your hand? I was able to get my longshore job because of what you did. I would never have been able to do that except for the things you changed. I can never thank you enough."

I wanted to cry. I had actually made a difference in the life of someone—a total stranger. How many times can we say that?

There was another instance that showed me how tense I was and how much things had changed, even if I couldn't see it. I was having a really bad day, and I was griping at everything and everyone. This was toward the end of my career, so people viewed me as someone in power, even if I felt I didn't have any. I was in the office and really feeling uptight.

"When are the truck drivers going to learn how to do things right? It isn't hard. Why can't they get it?" I snapped.

"Linda?" A guy I barely knew called out to me.

"What!" I yelled.

"Would you like a Jolly Bear?" He was holding out a bag of candy he'd gotten from the vending machine.

"What? What are you talking about?"

"You know, a Jolly Bear! They jolly you up when you're being a bear!"

I stood there looking at this guy grinning like the Cheshire Cat and holding out a bag for me to take. What he'd said was so hilarious that we all busted up laughing. It was a laugh I really needed, and I still remember what he did to get me out of my bad mood, even after all these years.

Another major change was in the pick process. Instead of the dispatcher giving jobs based on favoritism—or, in my case, based on prejudice against women—a computer made random assignments to the workers. It was a fair and logical system. The whole complexion of the dock changed over time. The change was probably slower than it should have been, but it evolved into an improved working environment that better matched the rest of the West Coast. Old guard slowly retired, and new workers joined and supported fair and just union operations.

It's so important that we remember the past so we don't make the same mistakes in the future. Learning from history is the best way to make today's world better. I didn't bring about change on my own, but I made a difference. That's all any of us can do. Stand up and make the world better, one day at a time.

CONCLUSION

In the end, I did what I set out to do. I kept my promise to my stepfather: I became a longshorewoman. I believe that I and the other women who stood up to management with me made the union and our community a better place.

Casual workers who the union had considered too old for promotion were taken care of as a result of the lawsuit. Many of them were promoted to "B" status and had retirement benefits backdated to much earlier in their careers.

One poor casual that I met years earlier had only one tooth in his mouth. After I got to know him better, I asked him why he hadn't gotten some dental care. He said it was because he didn't make enough money and, as a casual, he didn't qualify for medical insurance. He finally lost his last tooth. Sometime after the lawsuit, I met him again, and he had a full set of dentures. He was very happy about it, and I'm sure his health was better because of the dental care.

I believe I kept my promise to my daughter—that I would do everything in my power to make sure nothing happened to her like the things that happened to me. Of course, we can't ensure our children's lives are pain free. What we can do is leave the world a better place and tackle the most egregious issues first. I feel I did that.

Also, I kept my promise to myself. I broke the cycle that I was born into and became a stronger person for it. I'd like to think my life is at least a partial guide on how to approach difficulties, no matter where you find them in life.

My strong religious feelings have guided me in life. As I've held to those religious beliefs, I hope my life has been a mirror that shows a Higher Power is present in our lives, no matter how anyone sees that power.

This book is about more than women's rights. It's about equal rights for all workers. We all belong to the human race. African American rights are human rights. Hispanic rights are human rights. And women's rights are human rights. No one should be excluded because of who he or she is or where the person came from.

As my story has shown, companies must aim to do more than make a good profit. Sure, businesses need to watch the bottom line, but if they do that at the expense of fair and equitable treatment of their workers, in the end, that bottom line will suffer. Looking only at their profit without regard to how they treat their employees will cause some to suffer and eventually hurt the whole company. When one group suffers so another group can have more dollars, that unfairness eventually bubbles to the surface and explodes. People will suffer for only so long. And on a very basic level, such unfair treatment as the other women and I received just is not the right way to operate. It's certainly not practicing the Golden Rule.

We're supposed to live our convictions 24/7, and that doesn't need a special building or special ceremonies. The Jesus of the New Testament that I am familiar with didn't need a specific place, time, or reason to do good works.

I think it is entirely possible that an angel helped my stepfather out of his truck on the day of his accident and even came back and talked my father into convincing me to become a longshoreman. Otherwise, why all the fuss? Why did Bob make such a big deal out if it? I don't know, and I can't imagine the reason . . . unless you, the reader, are the reason.

Perhaps you're going to face a challenge so much harder and larger than the one I did. Maybe you need this book to show you the way. If that is the case and I have helped you understand how to navigate the challenges of life in some small way, then I am eternally grateful. Thank you from the bottom of my heart.

GLOSSARY

"A" man. A longshoreman with full membership.

agreement. A contract between a union and employer. It states wage rates, hours, and conditions and methods for settling grievances.

"B" man. Longshoreman dispatched after all "A" men. "B" men pay equivalent union dues but are not full union members.

bulk cargo. Grain, ore, liquids, or other freight that is usually not moved within sacks or containers.

business agent. The union representative to the workers of the union.

casual. An extra worker, meant to be used when all "A" and "B" workers have been assigned jobs.

clerk. Administrative position responsible for data entry of shipment information.

checker. The person who makes a written record of shipments as they enter the port and gives the data to the clerk or supervisor for entry.

collective bargaining. The process of negotiating a contract or settling grievances between management and employees.

container. An enclosed box, used for transporting cargo to and from the ship.

discrimination. Unequal treatment of workers because of race, nationality, religion, sex, sexual preference, age, or union activity.

dispatcher. Union official who assigns work to "A," "B," and casual workers.

dock crane. Used to move containers on and off ships.

dog. Manual lock to attach container to flatbed or to another container on board ship.

forklift. A motorized vehicle that lifts material stacked on a pallet.

grievance. A dispute between a worker and the union or management over a situation in the workplace or interpretation of a contract.

hustler. Small semi-tractor used to move trailers on the docks.

injunction. A court order prohibiting an action.

local, or local union. A labor organization based on workers performing similar kinds of work. It pertains to one location, such as Tacoma in this narrative.

longshoreman. During the nineteenth century, the term referred to workers handling cargo on the docks, in contrast to the stevedores and riggers who worked on the ship. Since the twentieth century, it means the workers who load and unload the cargo and then truck the cargo on the piers.

pick. The process of assigning longshoremen to jobs.

rigger. A worker onboard ship who attaches lines to cargo.

roll-on/roll-off. Loading and unloading wheeled containers through a side door of a ship.

ship's mate. A member of the ship's crew.

stevedore. During the nineteenth century, a worker who stowed or unloaded cargo within the ship.

strad. A motor-driven vehicle that straddles a container to lift and move it.

www.ingramcontent.com/pod-product-compliance
Lightning Source LLC
Chambersburg PA
CBHW030524080526
44586CB00011B/311